P9-DDJ-397

GUILT-FREE PARENTING

Guilt~Free PARENTING

Robert & Debra Bruce
Ellen W. Oldacre

DIMENSIONS
FOR LIVING

NASHVILLE

GUILT-FREE PARENTING

Copyright © 1997 by Dimensions for Living

All rights reserved.
No part of this work may be reproduced or transmitted in any form or by any means, electronic or mechanical, including photocopying and recording, or by any information storage or retrieval system, except as may be expressly permitted by the 1976 Copyright Act or in writing from the publisher. Requests for permission should be addressed to Dimensions for Living, P.O. Box 801, 201 Eighth Avenue South, Nashville, TN 37202-0801.

This book is printed on recycled, acid-free, elemental–chlorine-free paper.

Library of Congress Cataloging-in-Publication Data

Bruce, Robert G., 1949-
    Guilt-free parenting / Robert & Debra Bruce, Ellen W. Oldacre.
      p.   cm.
    ISBN 0-687-05994-1
    1. Parents—Religious life.   2. Parenting—Religious aspects—Christianity.   3. Guilt—Religious aspects—Christianity.
I. Bruce, Debra Fulghum, 1951- . II. Oldacre, Ellen W.
III. Title.
BV4529.B78   1997
248.8 ' 45—dc21   97-19480
                                                         CIP

Scripture quotations noted NIV are taken from the Holy Bible: *New International Version.* Copyright © 1973, 1978, 1984 by the International Bible Society. Used by permission of Zondervan Bible Publishers.

Scripture quotations noted RSV are from the Revised Standard Version of the Bible, copyright 1946, 1952, 1971 by the Division of Christian Education of the National Council of the Churches of Christ in the USA. Used by permission.

Scripture quotations noted JBP are from *The New Testament in Modern English*, by J. B. Phillips. Copyright © 1972 by J. B. Phillips.

Scripture quotations noted CEV are from the *Contemporary English Version* copyright © American Bible Society 1991, 1992.

Scripture quotations noted TLB are from *The Living Bible*, copyright © 1971 by Tyndale House Publishers, Wheaton, Illinois. Used by permission.

97 98 99 00 01 02 03 04 05 06 —10 9 8 7 6 5 4 3 2 1

MANUFACTURED IN THE UNITED STATES OF AMERICA

To our children:

Rob, Brittnye, and Ashley

Stuart and Emily

CONTENTS

PREFACE

*A*s Christian parents, we share a common call from God to minister to families. We also share a common expertise in dealing with parents through years of writing, teaching, and ministry experiences. Most important, we share a common journey of actually "parenting by guilt" as we strive to give more, do more, and be more for our children.

In keeping with this call and ministry, we wrote this book to offer practical, easy-to-apply suggestions to help parents get in control of their lives as they learn to lean on God's grace instead of living with unnecessary guilt about life's imperfections.

We know that our own personal parenting errors are being duplicated in today's young families, who are challenged by a faster-paced, high-tech lifestyle. Yet we know there are still only twenty-four hours in one day! Our mission? To help save families—families we see being manipulated by a "false god of guilt"—perpetuated by their peers, their own self-doubt, a lack of commitment to spiritual maturity, and greed. Sadly, our places of service allow us to see how even the church can unknowingly support parenting by guilt.

It is our conviction that guilty parents produce guilty children. However, the good news is that this vicious cycle can be broken. The ideas in this book are shared to help motivate, educate, and energize parents to change from "parenting by guilt" to "parenting by grace," so that we do not raise another guilty generation who reach midlife feeling lonely, empty, and ultimately burned out.

We know there is a better way to live and love. As you read this book, it is our prayer that you will take to heart our message on ending unnecessary parenting guilt and apply it to your life. We pray that you will ask God to guide your parenting journey into His path of inner peace and contentment.

> In Christ's name,
> Robert and Debra Bruce
> Ellen W. Oldacre

Chapter 1

The Verdict:
Guilty or Not Guilty?

*I*sn't parenting guilt a normal feeling?" Jack questioned. "When I look around and see what my peers are providing for their children, I feel like a failure. I can't compete on my salary."

Missy, the young mother of a toddler and newborn, added: "My guilt escalates through the day. I feel like I should go back to work to help pay the bills, but then I can't even think of putting the girls in day care. I suffer with so much anxiety from this conflict that I don't even enjoy the time being at home, which adds to my guilt."

"I feel guilty that my job keeps me from being home at dinnertime with Randy and the boys," said Betsy, an emergency room nurse who works the night shift. "But we need the money, and I've worked here for more than twelve years. I can't afford to quit."

Do you suffer from parenting guilt? Most mothers and fathers today identify with this feeling at some time. As working parents, we (Robert, Debra, and Ellen) know that it is easy to feel overwhelmed from parenting guilt. Robert and Debra feel guilty when deadlines are fast approaching, nights are filled with long committee meetings, and their teens are searching for clean socks while asking for the pizza delivery number—for the third night in a row. Ellen experiences similar guilt as she works all day, then comes home to two hungry teens and her husband, who also works all day and often travels.

In our minds we know we are dedicated Christian parents and are doing our best to provide for our families; however, guilt continues to tug at our hearts. Something continually nags at us that we must do more, give more, and be more for our children.

We firmly believe that guilty parents produce guilty children. But there is good news: The vicious cycle *can* be broken. You can break free from the "false god of guilt" and learn to live guilt-free, leaning on God's grace, and this book will help you to do just that.

Whatever Happened to Twenty-four Hours?

Rick, an accountant with his own business and the father of two preschoolers, tells of living with this guilt daily:

> I work ten-hour days, seven days a week during tax season to make payments on my new home and to keep our children in private school. The only time I don't feel guilt is after April 15, when I take some time off to be with my family. But that is short-lived because the rat race starts all over in September, and I feel guilty for the rest of the year because I've missed seeing my kids grow up.

Carolyn, a successful attorney and mother of two preteens and a preschooler, said this:

> Guilt is my middle name. Seriously, I get up an hour early every morning to exercise before making breakfast and

lunches. Then I rush the kids out the door to school and drive thirty minutes in heavy traffic to the law office. By the time I get to work and begin seeing clients, I envision ominous scenes of what I left behind at home—mountains of dirty laundry, a sink full of dishes from the night before, and globs of peanut butter stuck to the kitchen counter. Some days I even panic, thinking that I forgot to get my youngest in her car pool.

Is the guilt you feel as frustrating as that Rick and Carolyn describe? You are not alone. Through our many years of working with parents in the local church and community, we have observed that even the most dedicated parents are united by this common thread called *parenting guilt.* Parenting guilt is not age-specific; in fact, it can escalate the older your children get—if you don't get control of it. To understand the cause of this common discontent, let's compare where many of today's parents came from to where we are today.

Changing Times

Many of today's parents grew up in a time of relative prosperity, a time when education was of paramount importance to families (studies show that today's twenty-five- to forty-five-year-olds are the most well-educated group in history), when separation and divorce were much less common than they are today, when more women stayed at home than worked outside the home, and when extended family members—grandparents, aunts, and uncles—were more likely to live nearby for support. Family values and personal standards were stronger, and church attendance was a familiar family affair. Neighborhoods were safer, crime was lower, and many people didn't even feel the need to lock their doors.

Jewel, a retired mother of three and grandmother of eleven, who stayed home to raise her children during the fifties and sixties, shared her thoughts on raising a family during that time:

> Although I worked in an office before we were married, when our first child was born, I chose to stay home. Working mothers were uncommon then. We bought a small home when the girls were young, owned one car, and lived on a limited budget during their formative years, yet love and creativity flourished. Living on credit was something people didn't do at that time! Our girls never felt deprived because my husband and I always made whatever it was they needed. Likewise, we were very proud of their ability to be innovative, creative, and independent.
>
> Even though our funds were limited, with only one parent working, we were still able to take an annual family vacation and spend weekends traveling, going on picnics in the country, playing board games, or visiting relatives. You might say that we had more time for each other because there were no diversions such as video games, computers, or shopping malls.
>
> In retrospect, I'm very thankful I was able to be a stay-at-home mom when our children were growing up. I never experienced the kind of guilt that many parents today speak of. I mean, I was at home with my children day and night and was in touch with every facet of their lives: spiritual, physical, emotional, and intellectual.

Since the trend of stay-at-home moms of the past, as Jewel describes, times have vastly changed. With regular economic swings, making a living today is difficult for most and often requires that both parents work. The statistics are staggering. At this date there are more than 14 million working married couples with children under the age of eighteen in the United States, according to the U.S. Census Bureau. Not only do they work long hours every day, but they also come home to a second job of raising children. When you combine the responsibilities of making a living with raising responsible children, maintaining a solid marriage, and being altruistic by volunteering in the church and community, is it any wonder that everyone we speak with tells of experiencing parenting guilt?

"There just never seems to be enough time, energy, or money to give to our children," Jill said, "at least according to what we think they need." This lack of time, energy, and money, coupled with society's pressure to raise perfect children despite challenges and threats such as a mobile society, a devaluing of church attendance and family values, and increasing crime and violence, is creating an obstacle for many parents that results in immobilizing guilt.

A Painful Reality

Any parent today will tell you that *guilt* is the one word that is synonymous with raising children. For most of us, this anxious feeling begins before a child is born as we worry about prenatal care, our newborn's health, living conditions, educational costs, and even our child's playmates. Unfortunately, our list of concerns only increases after our children are born.

In the past twenty years, parenting has taken on new dimensions with the rise of two-career families. Sheila, a dental hygienist and mother of two middle school children, tells of feeling guilty for leaving her daughters at home alone after school:

> I started back to work twelve years ago after my youngest was born. We wanted our girls to have this beautiful home. Now my husband and I work such long days that we never seem to enjoy our home with the girls. We've missed

watching our daughters grow up, but our house payment takes up every penny.

Meredith, a stay-at-home mom, tells of living with guilt ever since she found out that her only child, Jered, has learning disabilities. While doctors have assured her that Jered's learning disabilities were not caused by anything she did, Meredith continues to blame herself. "I've punished myself for years for Jered's learning problems," she said. "Every time he has difficulty in a class, I blame myself."

Other parents we have spoken with tell of suffering from guilt for a variety of reasons:

* We both have to work in order to afford our child's private school.

* I'm divorced, and I never have enough energy to do all I should be doing with my son.

* I feel guilty for going back to work too soon after my son was born.

* We don't have enough family time because we both work long hours.

* My child cannot keep up with his peers, and I wonder if I'm somehow responsible.

* I feel guilty that my son has to go to public school instead of private school.

* I feel guilty because I missed my daughter's dance recital two years ago, and I cannot forgive myself.

* My daughter is overweight, and I feel guilty about what I might have done or not done to prevent it.

* We both lose our tempers after work because we are so tired, and I always regret it later.

* I chose to stay home with my children, and I feel guilty for sometimes being lonely and bored.

* We took a large salary cut for me to stay home, and our children complain that we don't eat out or go to movies as we used to.

* We can't afford a big home for our family.

* My three-year-old son is developmentally delayed, and I'm afraid that my friends think I'm a bad mother.

Parenting guilt is often counterproductive, leading to overwork, exhaustion, and anxiety. In fact, there is probably no more destructive human emotion than guilt. Some people live their entire lives in constant fear that their "misdeed" will be discovered or will reap unforgivable consequences. Guilt is a toxic form of self-hate in which the virtuous part of the personality accuses the guilty portion. The usual result is an all-pervasive, generalized anxiety. In some persons, guilt manifests itself as depression. In others, it expresses itself as an inferiority complex, for in one sense, guilt and low self-esteem produce similar feelings. In any case, guilt brings needless shame and, when felt for a long enough period, results in feelings of inferiority.[1]

A Woman's Concern

Both men and women experience guilt and its negative consequences, to be sure. However, parenting guilt is largely a woman's issue, as we will explain. But before doing so, it is important to recognize that many men experience the same sense of conflict yet may hesitate to recognize or admit the feeling. Perhaps that is because many were taught as young boys to hold back feelings of inferiority. No matter what the reason, more men are admitting that they do experience guilt and need some practical handles in alleviating this negative emotion in order to fully celebrate their lives as Christians.

As the senior pastor of a large church, Robert tells of feeling this guilt daily:

> There is always one more person who needs to be counseled; one more committee meeting to attend; one more sermon to write. And on those nights when I work late, I constantly think about how I need to be home with Deb and the kids. It's as if I have a constant tug-of-war going on in my mind day and night.

Though parenting guilt certainly is a reality among men, women tend to experience the guilty parent syndrome more often because our society has held "motherhood" in such high esteem, perpetuating such images as portrayed by the TV mothers of the fifties and sixties. Women not only feel intense pressure to have perfect marriages and immaculate homes and successful careers, but they also are expected to prepare "proper" meals, devote themselves to their children, volunteer in the church and community, and care for aging parents.

Where Is Wonder Woman When You Need Her?

It is easy to comprehend this guilt that goes hand in hand with being a working mother, causing perpetual unease and tension. Think about it. For most women, the message we have received from society is that not only should we receive a higher education and develop our talents as teachers, doctors, secretaries, artists, or lawyers, but we also better make sure that our children are bright, neatly dressed, and obedient, and that the house passes the "white glove test," too.

Only a mythical character such as Wonder Woman would be capable of the caretaking feats expected of today's mother. But oftentimes, whether we like it or not, we diligently follow the pattern of Wonder Woman despite changes in society. Life is just not as easy as it used to be.

According to the most recent Bureau of Labor Statistics figures, approximately 56 percent of all women with children under age six are working mothers. The numbers are even higher for mothers of children ages six to seventeen. About 73 percent of these mothers work. Statistics provided by the Bureau of National Affairs indicate that the number of working women with children under age one has increased 62 percent in the last decade.

Yesterday's Parent	Today's Parent
* mother cares for child	* mother cares for child or shared parenting
* father major breadwinner	* father and mother both breadwinners
* one-income family	* dual incomes
* mother does household chores	* mother does chores or shared chores
* marriage at an early age	* marriage postponed until after education
* children at an early age	* children postponed to build careers
* two-parent families	* two-parent families/blended families/ single-parent families

Women today can certainly relate to the saying, "You've come a long way, baby!" Yes, today's woman has more opportunities than ever before. In the midst of these opportunities, women can still be mothers, giving birth to children and nurturing them into responsible adulthood. However, the problem arises when the role of the traditional mother remains unchanged as women go into the workforce, whether because of financial reasons or personal desire. Women who stay at home to manage a family along with a home-based business also feel the impact of trying to do it all.

How can we do it all? We can't. That is when parenting guilt rears its ugly head.

Getting Off the Fast Track

Although times have changed, some things have remained the same. Statistics show that most women today work outside the home, either part-time or full-time, yet according to recent studies, women still do *80 percent of the housework* whether they are employed or not. When the responsibilities of working, raising children, and maintaining a home become too demanding, one person usually suffers: the mother. While our society has accepted the new role of women in the workforce, it is not so willing to alter the role of "perfect wife, mother, and homemaker." This adds to the frenetic fast track that we find ourselves on daily. Generally speaking, it is assumed that the woman who is not overworked does not take herself or her job seriously. We hope this book will help us to move beyond this misconception as we encourage personal caring for both men and women.

The fast track is just that: a fast track. Not only does it feel fast to you, but in most cases, it also feels that way to your family. Some women can do truckloads of work, yet they do not feel stressed or intrude on their family relationships. Others may only do half as much and not cope well with that amount. Only you can decide if your daily load needs adjustment. If you are short and irritable with your spouse and family, if you feel that they prevent you from completing your tasks and goals, it may be time to rethink the priorities in your life.[2]

We contend that we *do not* have to literally work ourselves into acceptance by others. Rather, we have to learn to accept ourselves and do what we can to be a "good enough" person—whether wife or husband, mother or father, employee or employer. Allowing ourselves to stay on the fast track with no reprieve creates physical and psychological problems (see chapter 2). Life is too short to continually live with negative emotions!

The Overachiever Parent

In addition to working harder than they ever have before, most parents say they are still trying to raise "perfect" children. This unrealistic attitude puts more pressure on parents, resulting in overscheduled and overstructured homes.

Amy and Jim are representative of many parents today and take pride in their children. Amy teaches at her church's weekday preschool program and is home by 3:00 P.M., when nine-year-old Jamie and twelve-year-old Marnie get off the school bus. After work, Jim coaches Jamie's Little League team and helps with Marnie's swim team at the local YMCA, while Amy carpools the children to piano and gymnastic lessons. Both Amy and Jim are active in their Parent-Teacher Organization, and together they teach Marnie's seventh-grade Sunday school class. They seem to have it all together—a loving Christian family with respectful children, a nice home in the suburbs, and enough money to live comfortably. Why, then, do they feel so guilty?

"My children are my life," Amy says, "but I worry that I am not doing enough to help them be successful. After I teach, I fill the rest of my day with volunteering at their school, checking into new activity classes for them, and making nutritious meals. I want them to have the background that helps them stay ahead. But I worry daily that I should do something more."

Jim agrees: "We want Marnie and Jamie to have every opportunity that we didn't have. But our hectic afternoon and weekend schedule of sports teams, lessons, and meetings is getting the best of us. I feel like we need permission to slow down and enjoy our family instead of constantly feeling guilty that we aren't doing enough as parents."

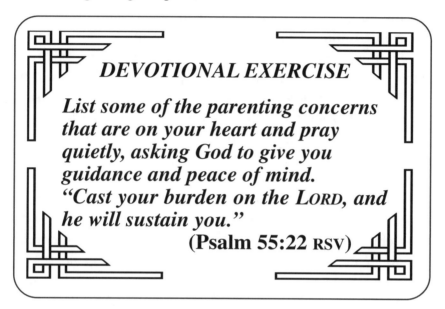

DEVOTIONAL EXERCISE

List some of the parenting concerns that are on your heart and pray quietly, asking God to give you guidance and peace of mind.
"Cast your burden on the LORD, and he will sustain you."
(Psalm 55:22 RSV)

Our friend Liz, a stay-at-home mom, compensates for her parenting guilt by overcommitting herself to everyone. After preparing a nutritious breakfast for her family, she goes with her daughters to school where she volunteers to run the school's clinic—five days a week. Liz leads a Bible study group each Thursday night, directs a children's choir at church, spends evenings carpooling her daughters to Scouts and piano, and takes dinner to her elderly father. As if this is not enough, Liz has enrolled in a night course at a local university to update her teaching certificate.

Though all of her commitments to children, family, church, and community are certainly admirable, Liz might be considered an "overachiever" as a parent. She tells of feeling lonely and unfulfilled as she constantly gives to others.

Like Liz, other overachiever moms tell of feeling guilty when their homes are not immaculate or their children fail to meet society's standard of perfection. "When Micah failed to pass the test for the gifted program at her elementary school, I thought I was going to die," Catherine said. "All of my friends' children were in this program. Where did I go wrong with Micah?" Some fathers also suffer from the same type of guilt. Steve told us what happened when his only son, Chad, experienced disappointment: "When Chad didn't get selected for the top Little League baseball team, I almost cried. Chad was fine and talked about going out for the team the next year. But I was devastated and felt like a failure as a father."

When parents are driven by their own and others' unrealistic expectations, not only do they suffer from loss of self, but also their children experience the loss of childhood as their well-meaning parents rush from one activity to another in an attempt to be perfect parents of perfect children. But the truth is that "perfect parenting" is a goal that is unattainable as well as unreasonable, and striving for this goal results only in feelings of guilt. Accepting that each family is different just as each individual is different is the beginning of a hopeful change.

Your Family Script

Look around you and notice how every family has its own unique qualities. Which of the families from the following TV shows represent your family's style?

____ *Leave It to Beaver*
____ *Home Improvement*
____ *The Brady Bunch*
____ *The Flintstones*
____ *The Cosby Show*

____ *Step by Step*
____ *All in the Family*
____ *Father Knows Best*
____ *The Simpsons*
____ *Murphy Brown*
____ *The Waltons*
____ *Family Matters*
____ _____ (Other)

You may be like more than one of these on any given day. Remember, even Ward and June got upset on occasion; after all, Wally and little Beaver weren't perfect!

The problem arises when we hold high such unrealistic standards for ourselves and our children. While you may watch some television shows and think that your life will never "measure up," it's important to realize that you live in the real world. Real people have difficulty getting along, holding down jobs, making their children mind, and keeping busy schedules without getting stressed out. Real families argue at the dinner table, slam doors when they are angry, and often have outrageous expectations of one another.

Your family is unique, and that gives you a great advantage. No one has written your family script for you. It's perfectly all right if you forget your lines once in a while, because God has given you a "learning laboratory" where you can keep working at it—your home. God also has given you a clean slate—His grace—so that you may start over every day and enjoy life and family.

The Hopeful Advantage

We truly believe that every parent has some pain to claim and lives with unnecessary guilt feelings over "what should have been" or "what could have been." Sometimes we become comfortable with these feelings of guilt, even if they make us and our family miserable. We convince ourselves that we do not deserve to be happy or unique because of past failures or because of what we may not be able to provide for our children. In this respect, parenting guilt is similar to a spouse abuse situation. Even though the victim is hurting, it is easier to stay than to leave. In these situations, the victim usually is convinced that the emotional suffering is deserved.

Not only is parenting guilt destructive and toxic, but it also can detract from our witness as Christians. We all need to understand that every day is a gift from God, and spending time feeling guilty is like returning the present unopened. Yet there is hope for followers of Christ. The apostle Paul challenges us to be "imitators of Christ" as we walk in love as Christ has also loved us. With this good news is the ultimate secret to ridding ourselves of unnecessary guilt. That is, because we are loved, we can walk in love; we can put aside all feelings of guilt, anxiety, and inferiority and stand with confidence in Christ.

We are important persons in God's eyes because of what Christ

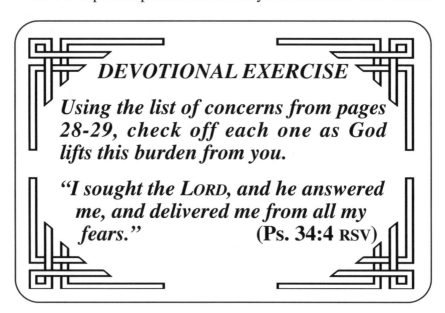

DEVOTIONAL EXERCISE

Using the list of concerns from pages 28-29, check off each one as God lifts this burden from you.

"I sought the LORD, and he answered me, and delivered me from all my fears."   *(Ps. 34:4 RSV)*

has done for us. No psychology text ever written can give us a better formula than God's Holy Word for dispelling the guilt that causes us to be slaves to society's expectations of parents today. Throughout this book, we will be using the Bible for specific direction as we challenge you to replace "parenting by guilt" with "parenting by grace."

Turn Over a New Leaf

Every person carries her own unique burden with guilt. But what are you going to do about it? If after recognizing the unnecessary guilt you live with, you continue to live with this emotion, it will only proceed to grow. Either you master the guilt, or it will master you. The good news is that bad habits can and must be broken, and parenting guilt can be stopped in its tracks—if you deal with this emotion right now.

Starting today, you can choose how to live your life—as a guilty parent or as a grace-full parent. We wrote this book to help you break the bondage of parenting guilt. Our goal? To liberate parents as we help you to let go of unnecessary guilt, respond to legitimate guilt by making changes or improvements in parenting skills, and maintain balance in your relationships while working toward being "good enough" in all that you do. Only by the power of God's grace can this happen.

We contend that parenting guilt does not have to be a reality. You can learn to move beyond this negative feeling into a life of freedom and hopeful possibilities through Christ Jesus as you remember to whom you belong.

Take a few minutes to complete the assessment on pages 28-29 to see what behaviors and attitudes may be causing you to experience parenting guilt, and then begin your journey through this book to guilt-free parenting.

Let's get started!

PARENTING GUILT INVENTORY

Look back over the past few months, then consider the following guilt-producing behaviors, attitudes, and expectations, answering either "yes" or "no."

Yes   No

____   ____   1. I sometimes wonder if I am unrealistic in my expectations of myself and my children at home, school, or play.

____   ____   2. If I make a mistake in parenting, I worry that my peers will look at me as a failure.

____   ____   3. Often I find myself losing control and reacting in anger when my child does something wrong.

____   ____   4. I believe that if I push my child hard enough to succeed at school and activities, he or she will have a better life.

____   ____   5. I feel embarrassed if my child "messes up" in school or in public (such as decisions or grades).

____   ____   6. I feel like a failure as a parent if I can't get my child to obey me much of the time.

____   ____   7. I often resent my spouse and feel as if I carry the load in the family.

____   ____   8. I sometimes dream of giving up because of the expectations and pressures I create for myself as a parent.

_____ _____ 9. I'm unsatisfied with myself if I feel my child is only average in his or her successes—in school or in extracurricular activities.

_____ _____ 10. If my child makes a mistake, I scold him or her immediately and then feel miserable.

_____ _____ 11. Even though it makes me uneasy, I/we depend frequently on credit cards to help make ends meet in our family.

_____ _____ 12. Though I might allow my child to miss church-related activities, I would never consider letting my child miss activities such as piano, ballet, gymnastics, or sports teams.

_____ _____ 13. I have high anxiety much of the time because my family life has not been as I would like it to be.

_____ _____ 14. I often blame myself when my child has problems with friends or a teacher.

_____ _____ 15. I often feel tired, overwrought, and harried and see no end to these feelings.

If you responded "yes" to more than three or four of these statements, it is time to reevaluate your parenting motivations, expectations, and skills and set some new priorities and goals. Start reading chapter 2 for a clarification of good guilt/bad guilt, then read on to find suggestions for making necessary lifestyle and parenting changes to dispel any unnecessary guilt that is keeping you captive.

Chapter 2

Good Guilt/Bad Guilt

When Shannon's employer offered her a large promotion, she was ecstatic. Shannon had worked for the same marketing agency for fourteen years, starting in the mail room and working her way up to middle management. However, when she found out that with the large salary increase came travel to nearby cities, along with overnight stays, she didn't know how to react.

"On the one hand, we sure could use the extra income to help pay for the private school tuition," she said. "Yet being away from the family several nights a week will be a strain."

Even though she had the support of her husband, Shannon postponed making a decision about the promotion for several weeks. She was unable to sleep at night for fear of making the wrong choice. Finally, when she realized how the temptation of extra money was taking over her life, she opted to say "no."

"I turned it over to God," she said. "After struggling with this decision for weeks, I realized that I had to look at it realistically.

The money was luring me to take a different role in the family, and that was not worth it to me."

Shannon is not alone. Both men and women experience parenting guilt in epidemic proportions. However, it is important to understand that not all guilt is bad, as in Shannon's case. We all have experienced that positive or "good guilt" can motivate us for change. For example, you may feel guilty that you don't spend enough time with your child after school for valid reasons. This type of guilt can prompt you to reorganize your life and set new priorities to allow for more quality parent-child interaction.

On the other hand, negative or "bad guilt" can cause great distress and emotional baggage, such as when your child is the only one among her friends who doesn't get chosen for the special ensemble for the school musical. You worry that this will temper your child's self-esteem for life, and you take partial blame for her failure. This negative guilt becomes crippling and must be managed. If you are to put guilt in its place, you must first understand the differences between good guilt and bad guilt and how each affects you.

Good Guilt

Good guilt is a positive, motivating force in that it helps us live up to moral and ethical standards and inhibits antisocial behavior. It calls us to take action leading to positive results. This type of guilt has been likened to the subconscious—a strong inner voice that puts specific parameters around our conscious behavior, such as stopping us from lying, cheating, or stealing. The inner voice of good guilt demands that we keep our mouths closed when we would like to tell someone what we really think, yet we know the words are hurtful. It also makes us think before striking our child in a fit of anger. In that regard, a dose of good guilt can keep us on the Christian path with our thoughts and behavior and make us take responsibility for our misdeeds.

Debra says that this good guilt makes her take a break in her workday when Ashley gets home from school, knowing that mother-daughter time is important for both of them. Ellen claims that good guilt motivates her to spend more time studying Scripture—especially when she sees her daughter, Emily, getting up early to spend more time reading the Bible and keeping a spiritual journal. A dose of good guilt keeps Robert from overscheduling nightly meetings at church so that he can spend quality time with family.

To fully understand what we call good guilt, consider the following five guilt statements parents have shared with us:

1. I feel guilty when I don't listen to my child at night because I'm busy cooking dinner or I'm too tired to care.

2. I feel guilty because I'm going to school at night after working all day. As a single parent, I rarely see my child. She goes to day care during the day, and a sitter keeps her at night. She is always crying when she sees me leave.

3. I feel guilty because I drop my three children off at church and go back home to mow the lawn. The pastor keeps calling, asking me to come, and I feel horrible.

4. I feel guilty because my husband and I argue over finances in front of our children. It makes our children sad to see us fight, but often it is out of our control.

5. I feel guilty because we bought a new car. Now I have to work weekends to make the payments, and I rarely see my family.

All of these statements are perfect examples of what we call good guilt. Though the feelings might be painful, they nudge us to make decisions that affect those around us in positive ways. This type of guilt beckons us to deliberate on our behavior and ask for forgiveness, if necessary, as we change our parenting ways. For instance, in example 2, the single mother cannot relieve herself of guilt for leaving her toddler both day and night, and rightly so. To bring a child into the world mandates that we make decisions with that child's well-being in mind. Every child deserves to have a caring parent. Although the single mother must work to make ends meet, perhaps she could postpone furthering her education until her child is older, thus helping to alleviate this unnecessary guilt.

Likewise, in example 3, the parent who feels immeasurable guilt for dropping his children off at church and then going home to do yard work will not be able to rid himself of this feeling until he makes decisions that are best for his family. Yard work can wait; role modeling Christian stewardship by attending Sunday school and worship with family each week is a parenting task that cannot wait. It must be done while children are forming their impressions about faith and the family.

Good guilt is a gentle nudge from God. It is given intentionally from our heavenly Father to make us feel uncomfortable and to motivate us to do what we know to be best for all concerned. Feeling guilty for working weekends to pay for a new car is a perfect example. We should feel guilty if in the midst of keeping up with the Joneses, we are losing precious time in molding our children's lives.

There are times when good guilt motivates us to reconsider our parenting techniques. Such is the case when we may feel guilty for disciplining our children out of reactionary anger. This type of guilt encourages us to confess our wrongdoing, ask for forgiveness, and look for more positive ways to deal with our anger and our children.

Bad Guilt

Unlike good guilt, bad guilt is unproductive. It tells us that no matter how hard we try, we will *never* be good enough. It cuts through our hearts like a knife. It also can be detrimental to our health because it stems from an idealistic feeling that we are ultimately responsible for everything in our child's life— even things that can go wrong. Negative guilt provokes a constant guilty feeling, stripping us of life's pleasures.

"For ten years I have felt guilty for having to work outside the home," Mary Jane said. "My husband and I both teach school and work hard to make ends meet, but I've always experienced this dullness or sadness during the day when I drop my kids off at day care. To compensate for this, I virtually let them do anything they want at night so they will laugh and be happy."

Bad guilt, as Mary Jane describes, is destructive guilt, and it complicates the lives of millions of parents. Not only do these parents live with unbearable stress—including symptoms such as insomnia, irritability, inability to concentrate, weight gain or loss, high anxiety, sadness, loneliness, and more—but their children also suffer greatly when they respond by being lenient parents who offer little discipline.

Julie told of feeling bad guilt to the degree that she overcommitted herself to everyone for years. "I didn't want to hurt anyone," she said, "so every time someone would ask me to bake cookies, lead the fund-raising drive, or chair a committee at church, I would say 'yes.'" While altruism is a virtue, Julie found out quickly that overextending herself left no time for her husband and children. "My oversensitive nature almost wrecked my marriage. I was so willing to help others but then was too tired to help those I loved most. In the midst of saving the world, I had neglected my family."

For Julie, overcommitment became a way of seeking love and

acceptance from others. However, in the midst of her busyness, she sacrificed time with her family. Bad guilt can make us act in ways we dislike, do things we know are not right, and make purchases that we cannot afford. It can make us overcommit our time and energy or even give in to our children when we know we should not. What's more, if we do not recognize and deal with negative guilt early on, it nags at us, makes us feel anxious and fearful, and keeps us from experiencing ultimate freedom as Christians. We find ourselves living with feelings of fear and inferiority. We lose enjoyment in life as bad guilt cuts into the threads of our being, making us feel unworthy of love or success.

Annessa told us that when her son's teacher recommended that they retain him in kindergarten because of immaturity instead of promoting him to first grade, the guilt almost ruined her life. "I kept thinking, if only I were a better mother, this would not be happening," she said. "Then I spent hours going over in my mind ways to hurry up his development, even though I knew I could not control that."

Lynne, a working mother with two teenagers, also talked about living with guilt:

For years I have lived with the guilt of wanting my children to be perfect when I compare them with others. I'm always trying to buy them expensive new clothes or fussing at them about the way they walk or wear their hair. And the guilt does not stop there. I get visibly upset when my daughters eat junk food for fear that they will gain weight. Likewise, when they prefer to stay inside to read, I feel guilty and worry that my girls will not be popular. The problem with this guilt is that I cannot remember ever enjoying my children. I always feel tense or anxious, as if something isn't right.

Instead of allowing her daughters to be what God intended, Lynne had a plan for their lives that was unrealistic and unobtainable. Her longing for acceptance from others caused her a life of anxiety, stress, and shame.

Guilt Leads to Shame

Some psychologists claim that it is important to clarify the difference between guilt and shame. Guilt comes from within, such as when you fail to meet your personal expectations; shame involves other people, such as when you do not meet the standards of others. In this regard, so much of what we might label as "guilt" may, in fact, be shame resulting from the fear of what others may think of us.

Shame feels like a sudden severing of our connection with the outside world. It leaves us feeling emotionally naked and revealed as something other than what we thought we were. It breaks the bridges that bond us to one another and leaves us feeling vulnerable and alone. The feeling of belonging and being connected with others is basic to our sense of self, and shame temporarily destroys that sense. Shame is so powerful that it has been called the "master emotion." In fact, childhood experiences of shame can determine how we experience other emotions for the rest of our lives.[1]

Think about when you yell at your dog for chewing your slippers. Usually, the dog will appear very guilty and respond by hanging his head in shame or sticking his tail between his legs and hiding under the table. This is an accurate comparison of how human beings feel when guilt becomes obsessive and takes over their lives. They hang their heads and feel whipped as shame takes over and truth is ignored. When this happens, shame is a negative result of guilt.

On the other hand, like good guilt, shame sometimes can lead to a positive outcome. Sometimes we *need* to feel shame for our actions. In his book *Healing the Shame That Binds You* (Health Communications, 1988), John Bradshaw talks about healthy shame and says that we are limited; we need help; we are not God. Bradshaw concludes that when we know our limitations, we know that there is something greater. When a feeling of shame is justified, we must accept the feeling, turn to Christ, and ask forgiveness for our wrongdoing. When we do this, we acknowledge our humanness and enable ourselves to take steps to correct our behavior.

Another kind of shame is what might be called unexplained or undeserved shame. Some individuals, including parents who tell of suffering from bad guilt on a regular basis, seem to live with feelings of shame and anxiety for no apparent reason. Others may readily cite a reason, placing the blame on themselves, but the blame is undeserved. When such is the case, we must look further for the root of the problem.

Let's Blame Mama

There are reports that symptoms of stress are greatly on the increase among working mothers as they try to balance home, career, children, and more, only to realize that it is not easily done—and sometimes cannot be done. A significant contributor to the problem may be that, as psychologists have indicated, bad guilt traditionally makes women feel the blame when things go wrong. Perhaps this is because women are conditioned to be sensitive and connected to others and feel responsible for them. On the other hand, when things go right, women usually have difficulty accepting praise. It is our experience that within a group of men and women, the women usually are the first to stand up and say, "Oh, it's probably my fault."

Take the case of a child doing poorly in school. Both parents attend the meeting with the teacher. "Justin's grades have been

Consider the following bad guilt scenarios and the ways many mothers might react.

IT'S MY FAULT

Child's Action	*Mother's Reaction*
Jennifer got her grade lowered because she forgot her term paper.	It's my fault because I didn't remind her.
It rained on the day of the family picnic.	Why didn't I choose a different day?
Morgan didn't get into the college of choice.	If only I had sent her to a better high school or made her study more.
Dustin has developed severe allergies.	If I had breast-fed him longer, this would not have happened.
Mikie didn't make school patrol.	He would have been more responsible if I hadn't worked when he was in preschool.
There is no money for a family vacation.	I should have taken that part-time job last year.
Samuel is painfully shy.	I should have pushed him more to speak to people when he was younger.
Sarah Beth didn't make the all-star team.	It's my fault because I haven't been active in the Little League.

falling for the past month," the teacher states. "I think you should be aware of this." Immediately, the mother responds, "If only I had turned off the TV or put him to bed earlier. Maybe it was because I was working on that project for church, and I failed to study with him each night. Perhaps it was because he had that cold. I knew I should have taken him to the doctor."

The father, on the other hand, does not take the blame for the boy's failure. Following the tradition of most fathers—though certainly there are exceptions, as in the case of Steve in chapter 1—he accepts the facts, saying, "We'll talk to Justin tonight and get this figured out."

Whether or not this kind of response happens because women are more emotional and in tune with their children's feelings or because women feel judged for their roles as mothers, bad guilt does not solve anyone's problem. Yes, most women feel they are responsible for their children, but when mothers feel they must be "in control" of their children's lives, they only cause themselves personal harm by continually burdening themselves with guilt.

When Parenting Guilt Takes Its Toll

Regardless of its cause, ongoing parenting guilt can become so all-consuming that some parents feel a general sadness day and night. All of us experience moments of sadness, loneliness, pessimism, and uncertainty as a natural reaction to particular circumstances. Sometimes we say we feel down or depressed. However, when these feelings become pervasive, being triggered by the least incident or occurring without evident connection to any outside cause, the individual may be suffering from serious or chronic depression. At times there may be a sudden burst of tears that the person cannot explain, or the person may experience constant weepiness.

Depression generally occurs when negative thoughts com-

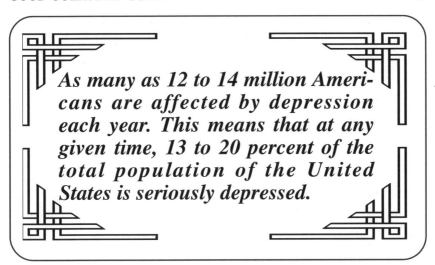

As many as 12 to 14 million Americans are affected by depression each year. This means that at any given time, 13 to 20 percent of the total population of the United States is seriously depressed.

pound upon themselves and get so rooted into the subconscious that the person cannot break out of the cycle of negativism and self-pity. If left untreated, it can last for months or even years, leading to feelings of helplessness and, at worst, suicide. Depression is not a sign of personal weakness or moral corruption. People can no more "pull themselves together" and get over depression than they can will away diabetes.

Depression can take several forms, from a major depressive episode to a chronic, low-grade depression called *dysthymia*. Dysthymia is defined as being in a depressed mood more days than not for at least two years and has few symptoms other than fatigue, low energy, and poor self-esteem.

Depression is a very debilitating, complicated affliction that is ruining life for millions of people today—twice as many women as men, according to most studies. Unfortunately, it is not as easy to deal with as other worries and stressors mentioned in this chapter. Many times depression can be "rooted" within a person, stemming from a biochemical imbalance or a symptom of an underlying ailment. In this instance, depression can be a cause of parenting guilt as well as an effect. Generally speaking, professional medical help is needed to maintain, control, and cure chronic depression with medication and therapy. Fortunately, many excellent prescription drugs and medical protocols can be of great assistance to persons suffering from serious depression. If you question whether you are seriously depressed, see your physician for an assessment.

Is There an Answer?

Whether the symptoms be chronic depression or occasional feelings of sadness, hopelessness, anxiety, or inferiority, parenting guilt affects us all at one time or another. So what is the answer to ending these feelings? Is there hope for those living with the stress of negative guilt feelings—even those who are striving to raise the "perfect child" in an immaculate home while pursuing an upwardly mobile career in the fast track?

Yes! There is hope. The answer lies in trusting Jesus Christ, for only He can relieve the unreasonable demands we place upon ourselves and turn our guilty feelings into guilt-free living. Only He can forgive our mistakes, our sins, and help us to set things right. When turning to Jesus for freedom from this life-wrenching emotion, we must cling to the truth taught in Matthew 6:34: "Therefore do not be anxious about tomorrow, for tomorrow will be anxious for itself. Let the day's own trouble be sufficient for the day" (RSV). We must learn to be "good enough" in all we do, knowing that in God's eyes we are not inferior. As Christian parents, we can admit our faults before God, confess our feelings of guilt, make necessary changes, and move on with the freedom we need to be productive disciples in a broken world. The following chapters offer specific and practical help for the journey.

GUILT-FREE CHALLENGES

1. Name a recent situation in which you felt "good guilt." How did this motivate you to make changes that positively affected your child's life?

2. Describe a situation in which you felt "bad guilt," or unwarranted guilt. What behaviors could have been changed to avoid this feeling? How did this negative guilt affect you? Your child?

3. How often do you feel guilty over something that went wrong while parenting? What situations usually increase these feelings?

4. Have you had a situation recently in which you blamed yourself for your child's failure or disappointment? Why did you feel responsible for this outcome? What do you think it would take for you to let go of negative guilt feelings, along with the accompanying stress?

5. Paul gives words of advice, telling us to practice the skills the Bible teaches. This practice is crucial for all of us as we try to nurture a spiritual journey apart from the church. When we work out, we do so by running, climbing stairs, swimming, doing aerobics, and more to get in touch with and develop the body. The same is true with spiritual disciplines such as Bible study, prayer, worship, and fellowship with other Christians. When we practice these "skills" regularly, we embrace our spiritual side and develop our relationship with God.

Start today by creating a quiet time calendar. Using a large calendar, schedule times each day for prayer and Bible study. This time is important as you get in the habit of building your spiritual "skills." Try not to allow any other commitment to interfere with this intimate moment with God.

Chapter 3

Permission to Be "Good Enough"

$\mathcal{L}$isa takes great pride in her four-year-old twins. With curly blonde ringlets tied up with matching hair bows, Caitlin and Carley look as if they could model for a fashion magazine. Mornings are spent participating in their church's preschool program. Lisa spends afternoons carpooling the preschoolers to kiddie gymnastics, preschool ballet, and Suzuki violin classes.

According to this young mother, she worries because the girls have already had symptoms of too much stress, such as Caitlin's complaining of stomachaches before classes and Carley's crying frequently at preschool. Still, Lisa continues the overly structured daily schedule for fear that "the girls will get behind their peers." In the midst of trying to raise perfect children, Lisa remains tired, harried, and tormented with constant insecurity, saying, "I'll never be good enough as a parent."

Haven't we all felt that way at one time or another? Perhaps you were just trying to make a memorable birthday cake for your child, and the center of the cake caved in while you iced it.

Hoping your child would not judge you unmercifully, you quickly filled the hole with whipped cream to hide your baking inadequacies. Maybe it was because your child didn't score in the top percentile on his exam at school, and you felt at fault for not making him study more. Or did you feel inadequate because you couldn't provide your family a new home or new car like your neighbors have? Even though you are working hard to meet the needs of your family, your efforts *never seem good enough.*

Nicki, a full-time nurse and the mother of an eight-year-old and a ten-year-old, said, "I become so tired and overextended trying to keep up with my kids that it begins to show up in my personality by the end of the week. I want everything that they do to go perfectly, including school behavior, grades, and extracurricular activities. The problem is that my attitude becomes less than loving when something goes wrong."

She told us of a time when her oldest son, who hated piano lessons, forgot his recital piece during a performance: "There I sat with tears running down my face as Sean stared blankly at the piano. The sad part of it was that deep down I was crying out of my embarrassment, not for Sean's."

Other parents like Nicki who try too hard to be perfect talk about being their hardest critics. "I begin to feel like a failure if my attempts at dealing with my two sons aren't perfect by my standards," said Tony, a social worker and father of two. "I reprimand myself in hopes that I will deal better with their behavior and conflicts. But I become so moody and angry inside that no one can stand to be around me. On paper, I know how I should act and react; it just doesn't always come out that way in real life."

This book *is* about real life and real people. If you are like Tony, Nicki, and many other high achievers, you want everything to be perfect. You take to heart Jesus' command to be perfect (Matt. 5:48). Not only do you strive for excellence in all you attempt, but you also want utmost perfection in all areas for

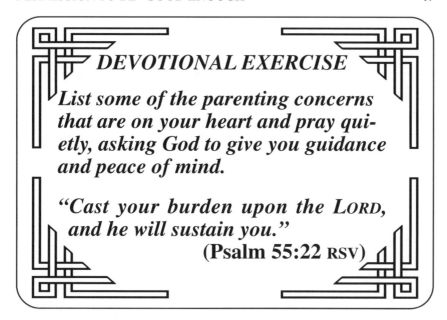

DEVOTIONAL EXERCISE

List some of the parenting concerns that are on your heart and pray quietly, asking God to give you guidance and peace of mind.

"Cast your burden upon the LORD, and he will sustain you."
(Psalm 55:22 RSV)

which you are responsible. Always struggling to achieve the best in whatever you do, you are driven to get ahead no matter what.

While your calling to Christian discipleship demands that you do your best, a constant push for perfection can cause negative guilt, leading to undue stress in you and your children. As you have learned by now, *negative guilt helps no one.* Whatever the cause of your feelings of inadequacy, it is important to realize that you don't have to be perfect. However, you do need to be "good enough." If you are nurturing your child spiritually and meeting his or her physical and emotional needs with caring and understanding, then you qualify as a *good enough* parent.

Good enough is a term we want you to become familiar with as you try to eliminate some of the unnecessary parenting guilt you may feel. You can learn to maintain balance in the family as you reevaluate your parenting situation, make some necessary adjustments, and learn when and where to draw the line, balancing personal and marital needs with the needs of your children.

A Hurry-Up Society

We know that, as humans, we are imperfect. Yet how many of us in our hurry-up society try to cram a week's worth of responsibilities into one day? Especially for "Kool-Aid Moms" who generously volunteer their days and nights to the church, community, and school, overcommitment can easily become a stumbling block.

Debra relates to this feeling of overcommitment and tells a story from her life:

Years ago at a young mother's study group I taught, I asked the members to pray for me to find strength in time management. "I can't prioritize my activities, and I feel like I'm out of control," I shared openly.

For several days after the meeting I earnestly prayed for each woman's specific needs: for Karen's daughter who was ill; for Joan's husband to find work; for Susan's marriage. I also waited patiently for my answer to prayer (well, as patient as I can be!). Two weeks went by, and I honestly anticipated this profound miracle to help me get my life in order. Meanwhile, I continued to fill my days with the usual long list of commitments to others, leaving no time for myself.

Then . . . God spoke. He answered my prayer and gave me ample time to evaluate my overcommitment with a rough case of the flu. I had the works—the high fever, chest cold, aches, and complaints. As I lay in bed moaning, Bob had to find other people to handle the many activities I was in charge of: the Brownie cookie sales, swim team awards dinner, adult choir retreat, children's choir rehearsal, the women's Bible study group. I remember crying with a thermometer propped under my tongue and the fragrance of Vicks VapoRub surrounding my blankets as I shivered with fever; I certainly wasn't thinking of anything but getting well.

I spent a total of eight days in bed and only the top priority items got completed: our three children were fed, bathed, hugged, and put to bed. As I recovered, I remained weak for another two weeks and moped around the house in my robe. It was interesting, though, how I began to appreciate the silence that went along with being alone. I started to read, daydream, and laugh more. Evenings were spent sitting with the family, talking, and playing games instead of running to night meetings at the church and school. My friends began to call to let me know that activities and organizations were functioning smoothly. The realization that I wasn't the only person who could lead the choir, teach the study group, and organize the community fund-raiser became apparent.

During my time-out before burnout, I think the real moment of awakening came when our younger daughter, Ashley, said with all honesty while lying beside me on the bed: "Mommy, I love you when you are sick. You have time to listen to me."

As Debra experienced, if you try to achieve perfection in all areas of your life, everyone will suffer. Trying to be perfect can become a form of trying to earn your way into God's favor, but in doing so you may block the grace of God in your life. Trying to be the perfect parent can be a burden when you don't allow yourself the risky necessity of making mistakes; and as parents, *we all make mistakes.*

The Bible recognizes perfectionism as an important issue for Christians. Jesus commanded us to be perfect, and Paul recognized our imperfection: "For our knowledge is imperfect and our prophecy is imperfect; but when the perfect comes, the imperfect will pass away" (1 Cor. 13:9-10 RSV). And in Philippians

3:7-14, Paul said that he was not already perfect, but that he was pressing on to become something more. Christians are to rate their ability with sober judgment, each according to the degree of faith apportioned by God to them (Rom. 12:3-8).

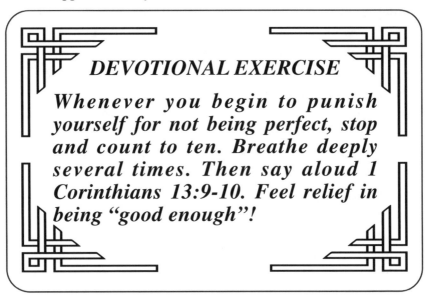

DEVOTIONAL EXERCISE

Whenever you begin to punish yourself for not being perfect, stop and count to ten. Breathe deeply several times. Then say aloud 1 Corinthians 13:9-10. Feel relief in being "good enough"!

As human beings, we are imperfect, and yet as a people of faith, we are pressing on to become something more than we are now. Knowing this tension, we can begin to make some important changes in our parenting expectations. These changes can help us to place parenting guilt in perspective so that we can enjoy God's grace at work as we seek wholeness and balance in all areas of life.

Perfect Parenting Is a Myth

Which of the statements on the next page can you identify with as you seek perfection in your life?

One of the biggest stumbling blocks of trying to be perfect is that parents develop unrealistic expectations of themselves and their children. These expectations can become self-defeating when events and persons outside your control thwart your perfection.

PERFECTIONISM QUIZ

1. ____ I must achieve my best, no matter how tired I feel.

2. ____ I cannot accept anything but perfection in all I do, or I criticize myself harshly.

3. ____ No matter how hard I try, I never feel that I've done enough or given enough.

4. ____ I would rather work at being perfect than spend pleasurable time with family and friends.

5. ____ I constantly reprimand myself and take partial blame when my children or spouse is not perfect.

6. __ I know that I am unrealistic in my expectations of myself in all parts of my life—at home, at church, at play.

7. __ When I make a mistake in my life, I fear that others look at me as a failure.

8. __ Losing control while dealing with others upsets me, and I have a difficult time forgiving myself.

9. __ If my family members don't use their time wisely, I feel responsible for not motivating them.

10. __ Sometimes I have thoughts of throwing in the towel because of the unrealistic pressure I create for myself.

Nowhere is it written that parents must do it all, that parents must be perfect. What's more, when we do try to fill the bill of perfection, something will give, whether our health, our well-being, or our relationships with family or even with God.

From our personal experience in raising children, we know that no matter how much you give, your life and your child's life still will not be perfect. You can bake all your meals from scratch, darn your child's socks, and volunteer in your child's school, but there still will be times when interruptions happen. There will be times when you are sick on the annual field day or burn the special dinner. You will make mistakes and be very imperfect. You must accept that as a parent, you are human. Once you can appreciate this fact, you can move on to enjoy your life and your child on an imperfect but loving level.

Respect Yourself

How many times have you said the following statements?

* I can never be good enough.

* I can never make enough money.

* I can never make my kids happy.

* I can never discipline them effectively.

The list goes on. Parents who are perfectionists have a difficult time when anything in their "perfect" family plan goes wrong. And if you have children, you know that things do go wrong—for change, interruptions, and mishaps seem to go hand in hand with raising kids. If you are a perfectionist, feelings of inadequacy abound. Yet to break the pattern of negative guilt, you must recognize the things you do right and affirm them.

Respect is important in order to live as a guilt-free parent, to feel the love and freedom that Christ Jesus can give. To respect yourself, you must acknowledge your gifts—yes, we all have special gifts from God!—and learn to lean on them, even when other parts of your life seem dismal.

A popular magazine ran a fascinating article several years ago about men and women who earn their living making extraordinary use of their natural senses. The article cited the practiced eye of a diamond inspector, the sense of feel of a wool inspector, the developed ear of a cymbal tester, the sense of smell of a fresh fish inspector, and the sense of taste of a milk-taster. All acknowledged that they had no special gift in the area of their senses. They had simply trained themselves to use what they had to a high degree.

As Christians, we make up a unique Body of Christ with different interests, talents, and skills. In the New Testament, Paul writes, "Having gifts that differ according to the grace given to us, let us use them: if prophecy, in proportion to our faith; if service, in our serving; he who teaches, in his teaching; he who exhorts, in his exhortation; he who contributes, in liberality; he who gives aid, with zeal; he who does acts of mercy, with cheerfulness" (Rom. 12:6-8 RSV). Because God has created us all in His image as unique individuals, there is a niche for everyone. We simply cannot stress that enough! We do not have the same fingerprints or footprints. Did you know that each of us even has a one-of-a kind tongue print? Yes, at the basic level of our existence, we are all unique.

Start with Affirmation

In the space that follows, write down your parenting strengths. Perhaps you pride yourself in being consistent with discipline. Maybe you have taken special time to teach your children Bible stories, and you feel confident about their faith walk with the Lord. Or maybe you are like most of us and feel good just because you made it through another day! Even if your greatest strength is waking your child up each day, preparing food for him, and making sure he gets on the school bus and does his homework at night, write that down. For many, that would be quite an accomplishment.

My Greatest Strengths as a Parent

1.

2.

3.

4.

5.

6.

7.

8.

9.

10.

Now, we want you to turn to this list and review these strengths every morning during your quiet time with God, thanking Him for these special gifts. As Christians, when we are able to build on our strengths, we can begin to accept areas in our lives that we have no control over. Isn't that a strength in itself—to accept our weaknesses? Personal weaknesses that used to haunt us with negative guilt are diminished if we allow God to walk with us daily.

Identify Guilty Feelings

Journaling can be an effective tool in our walk with God. Writing in a journal also can help to identify parenting guilt. Journaling lends itself to great self-inquiry, especially when feelings of guilt take over for no apparent reason. Whereas normal consciousness makes us aware of our identity and surroundings, journaling allows us to experience a higher plane of consciousness and, with the practice of self-discipline, enhanced awareness. We often hide from or are even unaware of intense feelings that guilt can bring, especially when we begin to compare ourselves with others. The intense self-inquiry of journaling can open the pathways leading to these destructive inner feelings and deepest concerns.

Because writing in a journal is more introspective than writing in a diary, you may choose to make this part of your quiet time with God. It will allow you the pleasure of beginning an intimate relationship with yourself and with God as you take time to evaluate your life, identify your feelings, and get in touch with how you react to life's pressures. Journaling also will enable you to identify reasons for procrastination as you unfold deeper motives, such as perfectionism or low self-esteem. By understanding the root causes of what motivates you, you will function more effectively, knowing ahead of time personal weaknesses that serve as stumbling blocks in your life.

Know When to Draw the Line

Feeling overwhelmed and questioning when to draw the line are normal. But before the feelings of guilt and resentment become a reality in your life, you must reevaluate your parenting situation and make necessary adjustments, balancing your personal needs with the needs of your children. No one, we repeat, *no one* can be an exceptional parent, a loving and loyal spouse, *and* a super employee or volunteer in the community without having balance in her or his life.

Margie, a single parent, could not release the negative guilt that had gripped her since the day she went back to work after her divorce two years ago. "I cry when I leave my daughters at nursery school," she said. "Then I feel sad all day thinking about how lonely they must be without me. After I pick them up, I feel guilty for leaving them all day and let them stay up late to show them I care."

Having to work outside the home, as Margie does, is not a reason for parenting guilt. Her work is vital to the family in order to pay for rent and food. Knowing this, she must learn to let go of the feelings of negative guilt and realize that she is being good enough as a parent. With this release, she can begin to feel confident that she is doing all she can to love her children, even though she is away during the day.

As you learn when to draw the line in your life, it is important to accept what you cannot change. It means accepting the child who may not be the kind of student you were, or adjusting to your income level, even if it isn't as high as your best friend's. It means letting some lesser things go, such as vacuuming every day or trying to work overtime, focusing instead on giving family members quality time and emotional support.

We are sure that when it is your time to meet your Maker, you won't be saying, "Gee, I wish I had scrubbed the counter more or stayed at work later each night to make a few more dollars." Taking charge and doing something about problem areas in your family's life are significant; knowing when to draw the line and accept life—with its ebb and flow—is the challenge of Christian parents.

Deal Openly with Those Who Cause You to Feel Guilty

Accepting the ebb and flow of life is much easier when we learn to deal openly with persons in our lives who cause us to feel guilty. Whether it is a well-meaning relative or a neighbor who seems to have it all, most of us can become undone by people who cause us to feel guilty.

"I thought we were doing great until Tom's mother started comparing our children to his sister's children," Terri said. "All I heard was Stephanie's children made better grades, were more talented, and had excellent manners compared to mine. I felt so dejected and was full of self-doubt—until I spoke with my sister-in-law, Stephanie. I was astounded to learn that Tom's mother was saying the same thing to her about our children, and that she was feeling unnecessary guilt, too!"

Another young mother, Patrice, told us that her best friend makes her feel inadequate in all she does. "Allison's home is immaculate, her children are quiet and obedient, and she looks perfect no matter what time of day," Patrice said. "It takes me all morning just to bathe the baby and get dressed. By the time Jonathan comes home from preschool for lunch, I'm ready for a nap." Though Allison never did anything intentional to make Patrice feel less than perfect, Patrice's inability to accept herself caused her to feel self-imposed guilt when she compared herself to Allison.

Someone, somewhere, will *always* cause you to feel guilty— whether intentionally or unintentionally. Someone will always have more, do more, and be more. Therefore, when you begin to feel the overwhelming feelings of anxiety from negative guilt, you must ask yourself if the guilt is self-imposed. Ask, Do I have any reason to feel guilty? If there are areas of your life that you need to work on, do so. If not, realize that you cannot change people around you, but you can change how you react to these people and how you act in your life. Only when you can do this will you begin to erase the negative guilt feelings and enjoy who you are as a child of God.

Allow Yourself to Be Average

Another way to erase negative guilt feelings is to allow yourself the privilege of being average in some areas of your life. It is OK to relax sometimes! Athletes attest to the fact that they excel in only a few sports because of the special development of the muscles required for each sport. Great golfers may be lousy football players. Good writers may not know how to bake a layer cake. Similarly, you don't have to be the perfect parent in all avenues of raising children.

As three parents who are *not* perfect, we feel that it is really OK to be average at some things in our lives. We have learned to focus on our strengths and feel good about this. In the Bruce home, Robert enjoys spending time with the kids playing sports, waterskiing, or diving for lobster. Debra, on the other hand, prefers spending time with the children in activities such as problem solving, creative brainstorming, or working on class projects. In Ellen's family, she enjoys teaching her children how to reach out to others as the family befriends a neighbor child or has international guests into the home. Her husband, John, enjoys learning interesting things about their teens by being the main family taxi driver, who often ends up with a carload of teenagers. Redirecting our thoughts and energies to our strengths helps us to eliminate our negative guilt.

Raise Good Enough Children

Think about it: How many times do we take our negative guilt out on our children only to make them feel guilty, too? The problem arises when our perfectionism causes us to go around feeling guilty and modeling guilt or modeling a lifestyle born out of guilt, helping to perpetuate this in our children. Not only must we give ourselves permission to be average in some areas of our lives, but we also must give our children the same permission—no strings attached. "But I want my child to be his best," you may say. "How can being average be acceptable?" We don't mean being average if your child has unused talent or is hiding his ability. But allowing your child to be good enough means knowing when *not* to push him harder when he is giving all he can.

Cure the Worry Wart

Some parents spend hours worrying about every aspect of their child's life without seeing the big picture. Worries prevail, such as:

* Did he eat enough or too much?

* Is she potty trained too early or too late?

* Will he make the team in high school if he doesn't start training at age three?

* Should I spend time teaching her to read before preschool?

* Will she get into college if she gets a B in handwriting— in first grade?

The problem with constantly worrying that a child is not performing perfectly is that we often fail to love the child at that moment for who she is—no strings attached. Instead, we love her for how she looks, what she achieves, or how well she sings, dances, or does cartwheels in gymnastics.

We cannot emphasize enough that as Christians, we are accepted by God right where we are in life—warts and all. God loves us even though we have faults, even though we are weak, even though we cannot sing, dance, or do cartwheels! God's love is so amazing that it's there for us when we lose our jobs, lose our friends, or even lose our spouses to divorce. We are loved with no strings attached—simply because.

To be good enough in our families, we must imitate this all-powerful and unconditional agape love that Jesus taught. We must embrace our children each day, whether we feel like it or not, and accept them on the spot. For it is only when we are accepting of others, faults and all, that we can be accepting of ourselves and let down perfectionistic barriers in our lives.

Learn to Laugh

Winston Churchill said, "It is my belief, you cannot deal with the most serious things in the world unless you understand the most amusing." Don't you agree that laughter helps you to relax and let go of problems? As you begin to accept your imperfections, learn to laugh at yourself—yes, even at your parenting skills.

Probably nothing is more difficult than to take yourself lightly. But to break the perfectionistic habit, you will need to stop taking every fault or mistake so seriously.

When the Bruces' son, Rob, was in elementary school, he sincerely asked his grandmother why she didn't send his mother to cooking school instead of writing school. Debra shares:

At first I was crushed. I knew that our meals were healthy. They just weren't in the same elite category as Grand-mommy's. After getting over the initial dejection, I learned to laugh about my one-dish meals. It became well-accepted

Which Describes Your Parenting Mood?

cheerful	depressed
pleasant	cantankerous
lighthearted	dull
amiable	grouchy
congenial	gloomy
good-natured	melancholy
harmonious	woeful

among family members that Mom's cooking was just good enough—and that was OK. We celebrated the books and articles that I wrote, and got by with my adequate cooking.

Ellen's family laughs about her directional skills. She can be the editor of two magazines and remember the names of people she has met from all over the world, but she has no conception of direction. Quite honestly, she is "scripturally correct," because her left hand seldom knows what her right hand is doing! She knows her left hand because that is where her wedding rings are. She gives directions by landmarks only. North, south, east, and west? These words are not even in her vocabulary. Her children can recall stopping at convenience stores and service stations all over the United States to get directions.

"It doesn't bother me anymore," jokes Ellen. "In fact, now I get very impatient with other people in my family (not naming any names, of course) who realize that they don't know where they are but refuse to stop and ask. Convenience store clerks are my best friends."

We laugh at our quirky inadequacies and give you permission right now to laugh aloud. Not just a timid chuckle, but a real belly laugh. Think of a humorous event in your life, put a smile on your face, and laugh until you cannot stop for thirty seconds. How did you feel after doing this exercise? Most will admit that taking time for a light moment, especially when they are worried or stressed, alleviates some of the tension in the body.

The ball is in your court. You can look at parenting in two ways—with increasing hope and optimism or with dreary thoughts of pessimism. How do you see your life? Do you take yourself so seriously that each day is a major effort? Or are you leaning toward the lighter side of life and finding simple pleasures in the daily happenings in your home? Remember, only you can make the changes necessary to start seeing life positively.

Grow Through Failure

We cannot reiterate enough that *guilt is counterproductive.* Guilt does not help you to be a better parent. Rather, it interferes with the pleasure of family life that you should experience. When you worry about what you cannot change, you waste time needlessly—time that you could spend on momentary pleasures with your child.

In learning to be good enough, we give you permission right now to fail. Although failure can lead to disappointment and depression if not handled in a positive way, it is the pathway to growth. Perfectionists need to interpret a failure not as a personal rejection, but as an opportunity to explore new avenues. Once you learn to risk failure and disappointment, you can begin to grow as a whole person, learning from life's ups and downs.

Many stories from the Bible teach us how others dealt with personal tragedies and rose above them. For example, Job's struggles give us insight into suffering and how faith in God can sustain us. During times of failure and disappointment, God offers us comforting assurance, loving forgiveness, and tremendous strength.

As you learn to be good enough as a parent, be willing to lean upon God. As we will share in the next chapter, God can fill any inadequacies or insecurities you feel in your life. God's grace forgives you and frees you to live with your imperfection. God's abounding love will strengthen you to move toward acceptance of yourself and your child.

Through daily prayer, Bible study, and fellowship with other Christians, you can remember God's presence and can know yourself to be loved for who you are, not for what you do or how well you do it. So, do you want to be the perfect parent? Or can you live with being good enough? If you do feel overwhelmed from trying to be perfect, start today to make plans to slow down, get your personal life in order, and let your child and yourself be good enough.

Permission granted!

GUILT-FREE CHALLENGES

1. Are you a perfectionist? Assess your personality using the quiz on page 51. To break the perfectionism habit, make sure that the amount of time you put into an activity or job is well worth the end result and does not produce any undesired consequences in your family life. Unless you can meet these criteria, back off and learn to be "good enough."

2. Does the thought of being "good enough" bother you? Some parents are not fulfilled unless they actively play the role of Wonder Woman or Super Dad. The reality is that *no one* can play this superhuman role without suffering in some way. Give yourself permission to be "good enough" in one or two areas, and evaluate your feelings after doing so. Are you able to relax and enjoy your life even more?

3. Are you a parent who spends hours worrying about every aspect of your child's life without seeing the big picture? What worries come to mind as you read this? Write some of these worries down on a sheet of paper, then ask, What can I do to relieve these worries? If you are unsure, talk it over with a trusted Christian friend. If they are needless worries, won't you let go and trust that God loves your child more than you do and will take care of him or her?

4. Start your "Guilt-Free Journal" today. Through this intimate journey, you can begin to peel through the layers of self and discover your "enemy within"—

negative beliefs about parenting or yourself that hold you back from enjoying life fully. This recording and reflection will enable you to gradually eliminate less desirable thoughts—such as envy, loneliness, depression, anger, and self-hatred—and begin to build your inner confidence as you seek new understanding.

5. Acknowledging one's faith in Jesus as Lord and Savior is the beginning of a personal relationship, a faith walk, with Him. Then, spiritual growth happens gradually, just like physical growth; it takes time for God to work in the life of the believer and create a new being. The problem occurs when we focus only on secular matters, such as materialism, and we lose sight of matters of the heart. When we are away from the church, we too easily forget the essential teachings of our Christian faith. Remember, our inner selves determine our destiny, and we must nourish this inner spirit each day to handle the guilt in our homes. As you seek to be good enough as a Christian parent, admit your faults to God in prayer, confess feelings of guilt, then move forward with the strength that only He can give.

Chapter 4

Peace Is a Person

*I*t happens to everyone. After an unusually tormenting day of trying to meet the needs of many, you stop right where you are and wonder, Why am I doing this?

Perhaps this awakening happened when you were hurrying your children to grab their backpacks, so that you could take them to school and still make that important client breakfast meeting. Maybe it occurred when you were doing some last minute shopping after picking up your children from day care, trying to get through the checkout line as they pleaded for another favorite candy or toy. Whenever your awakening took place, did this moment motivate you to search for a new perspective on life?

You probably have heard the expression, "The hurrieder I go, the behinder I get." Don't we all feel that way at some point in our lives? We race ahead in the fast lane, working long hours to make more money; motivating our children to make good grades in school while being responsible leaders, skilled athletes, and

popular friends; trying to keep up with those we envy by purchasing material goods we don't even want or need. Oh, yes, we
have it so good—or do we?

Drivenness = Destruction

As men and women who have been able to pursue higher
education and career advancement, we should be most satis-
fied. But we're not. As a generation with access to the latest
medical advances and technology, we should feel healthy and
vibrant. We usually don't. And as people who come home to
life in suburbia and new cars, VCRs, color television sets, sur-
round-sound stereos, CDs, IRAs, and stock portfolios, we
should be contented and secure. Maybe we're not. One must
wonder: If our lives appear so captivating—so together—why
are so many today experiencing the distressing anxiety of parenting guilt?

Look around you. For most parents, life is confused, disorga-
nized, frustrating and, to be honest, quite difficult. Most of us
feel imperiled as we suffer from feelings of guilt and inferiority.
It often seems next to impossible to experience the true joy and
freedom we know we should have as Christians, especially after
doing battle in today's world.

It is certainly no news to you that most of us are driven. We
are driven to acquire, driven to achieve, and driven to succeed.
(See chapter 6 for help in determining how driven you are.)
However, this drivenness is taking its toll, resulting in tremendous stress and guilt for millions.

Physicians used to say that 35 to 40 percent of the health
problems Americans faced were stress induced; newer studies
now indicate that stress could be responsible for as much as 60
to 80 percent of all physical problems. As we share in chapter 6,
these stress-related disorders include headaches, high blood

pressure, insomnia, back pain, muscle aches, and a host of psychiatric disorders.

The Quest for Inner Peace

If it isn't insomnia or a perpetual headache due to stressful living, most of us live with a constant nagging feeling that something is amiss. However, inner peace is not found on the fast track. We cannot buy it, win it, negotiate it, or inherit it. As many parents experience, a drivenness to find happiness results only in feelings of stress, anxiety, worry, and fear.

True inner peace can be found only one way: through a personal relationship with our Lord Jesus Christ. Only God through Christ can remove the stain we call guilt. We have experienced that knowing God through Jesus Christ can fill any inadequacies or insecurities we may feel in our lives; His grace forgives us and frees us to break the bondage of guilt.

Ellen admits to once living a fast-paced life filled with giving to others—until she realized that not only did she feel burned out and ineffective, but her relationship with God was not complete.

Ellen's Story

I was a high school student during the early seventies. Ironically, the symbol of the day was the peace sign. Kids wore it on T-shirts, sewed it on jackets, and spray painted it on buildings. As much as everyone said we wanted peace, the clothes, the government, and the culture were anything but peaceful. In looking back, it seemed like the nation went from June, Ward, and the Beaver to the Killing Fields—all at one time. The country's desperate pursuit for peace saw the increase in drug use, alcohol addiction, free sex, and political demonstrations.

I was never really bothered by the leading temptations of the day. My habits had already developed. My drug was "busyness." You see, I didn't have time for those "bad things" because I was always "doing," always leading others. I was so busy "doing" that my self-worth and approval became wrapped up in good activities. I was "the good girl doing good things." In fact, I felt tremendous guilt if I wasn't doing these good deeds.

Many of those things helped others, my family, and the church. And if others think they have discovered a "doer addict," they will continue to give the addict more to do.

My "doer" habit continued into adulthood. I was a Christian with a committed belief in Jesus Christ, but part of my misguided theology included the thinking that if I taught enough children's classes at church, loved my family enough, was room mother for each child enough times, read my Bible regularly, and prayed without ceasing, I would achieve acceptance and spiritual utopia or peace. Sadly, even though I received much praise for my ability to do so much at once, my pursuit of optimum peace just made me tired, feeling only temporary times of peacefulness.

I searched diligently for peace in my children, my parents, my church, and even the Bible. I felt sure that I was a spiritual failure because no matter how hard I tried, I couldn't find lasting peace.

"I've Got Peace Like a River" became a popular chorus during those times. Ironically, even though I sang it well, I could not live it. My song sounded more like "I've Got Peace Like a Pond." Indeed, at this busy time in my life, I felt as if my river had run dry.

For me, peace was not found in pleasing all the many people I had contact with or the constant activities. I finally discovered that I could not find peace by pursuing it, because peace is a person. Peace is the person of Jesus Christ. I had pursued peace instead of pursuing Christ. What a difference that makes! This is the difference between *trying* and *trusting*. Years later, I am now learning to experience peace because I am experiencing the Prince of Peace.

Were all my activities in vain? No, I believe God still used me. My busyness was not bad; it just was not the best. But God never gave up on me. He kept drawing me to the best. As A. W. Tozer wrote in his ever timely *The Pursuit of God*, "We pursue God because, and only because, He has first put an urge within us that spurs us to the pursuit. The impulse to pursue God originates with God, but the out-working of that impulse is our following hard after Him. All the time we are pursuing Him we are already in His hand."[1]

For those of us who are recovering "doers," trusting is risky business because it means we are not in control—God is. But the peace that comes from the assurance that I am in the right pursuit is worth the risk.

The most exciting part about following the Prince of Peace is that I have learned to relax. There are times now when I can actually do nothing—and not feel guilty! I now have a favorite TV show. I can take long walks with my family. I enjoy driving down the road with my kids in the car and turning up the radio really loud—and we sing with it! And believe it or not, I honestly say "no" to guilt when I haven't taken a cake to the new neighbor or cleaned the house in the past week.

Am I now busy with things that really matter? First of all, those relaxing activities really do matter. They give me the calm energy necessary to tackle the more strenuous activities. Second, I am now busy with the stuff God has given me to be good at, so that I can please Him. It took me years to accept myself and my gifts as God made me. I have to continuously be aware of the "lures."

A reverting tendency of a recovering "doer" is the comparison game. If I compare myself to other people I greatly admire, I will never measure up. I will never be able to cook as well as my mother, write as well as my friend Susan, or deal with people as well as my friend Selma. There will always be someone prettier, thinner, younger, wiser, and smarter than I am. There will always be someone who is a better parent than I am. But I have gifts that my friends don't have. No one else "flows" just like me when God is in control, and I am allowing Him to be my peace. And no one else "flows" just like you when you choose to pursue the Prince of Peace.

You might wonder how my busy schedule now is different from my busy schedule before. When I was running on my own energy, searching for acceptance and peace, I felt compelled, almost frantic, to try every activity, just in case it was the one that worked. Now I am careful not to get overloaded. If I am asked to participate in a major project at church, I begin praying for God to affirm through others and His Word that my gifts are matched for the tasks and that I should be involved. The wonderful benefit of knowing the Prince of Peace is that when a God-size task is before me, so is God. If He calls me to a particular task, He will be my stabilizer and strength giver to help me carry it out.

As I drive to work each day and begin to get overwhelmed by all that I must do, He draws me to Himself. I focus on God and thank Him that He is peace. I don't ask God for peace. I just ask to know Him better and deeper. I worship Him, and He invites me over and over again to be still and know that He is God.

As Ellen describes, real faith—real peace in life—is found only through a dynamic, forward-looking relationship with the Creator. Yes, true inner peace is found only through the person of Jesus Christ. You can experience this, too, as you plunge into a multidimensional walk of faith. When we refuse to venture out and take risks of faith, to stretch for what is beyond our grasp, we can miss out on the real exhilaration of life—God's serendipities—often finding ourselves disappointed and empty-handed.

Guilt Starts with Fear

Instead of finding the peace that Ellen tells about, most of us remain troubled, guilty, and afraid. As guilty parents, we have fears about our health, our children, and our careers. We are afraid that we cannot continue to keep up the pace we live, and that this will result in less income, which will spill over into our social lives as well as our personal lives. We worry that our children will not be successful, that they will not perform in school or get accepted to the proper college. We worry. We feel guilty. We live in fear.

Fear is one of the earliest emotions that a baby experiences, and all fears tend to be variations of three basic ones:

1. The fear of falling
2. The fear of loud noises
3. The fear of being abandoned

Most of us learn to deal with the first two, even though some of us may have problems with heights. The fear of falling may still be with us, but for most it is not debilitating. As we get older, we may not fear loud noises as we did as an infant, but they may bother us just the same. The fear of abandonment, however, is a subtle fear of which we may not even be aware, but which may get even more acute as the years pass. It is no fun being left alone.

A story is told of a large metropolitan hospital where there was a constant problem with noise in the infant nursery. Crying babies would disturb one another. The sound level was almost unbearable for the staff as well as the newborns. They tried separating the babies and soundproofing the walls. Although it helped the staff, it did not seem to calm the infants. Then someone had the bright idea of playing a recording of a mother's heartbeat beside each bed. It worked! The sound that the baby heard even before it was born was the sound that comforted it the most.

Psychiatrists used to talk about "birth trauma." What is that except the trauma of being separated and the subsequent fear of being abandoned? Perhaps we still carry that fear with us all of our lives. Maybe that is why we know no lasting peace until we reconnect ourselves with the Prince of Peace.

For many of us, fear is linked to guilt. Norman Vincent Peale tells of spending some time on a lush tropical isle in Jamaica. In the hotel where they were staying, a map hung in one of the hallways. In the corner of the map, there was some very faint lettering over an almost totally uninhabited part of the island. Looking closely, Dr. Peale realized that the words said, "The Land of Look-Behind."

Intrigued, he asked the owner of the hotel what those words meant. The hotel owner said that in the days of slavery, runaways from the sugar plantations sometimes escaped into that lonely and barren territory. They were often pursued by slave owners or the authorities with guns and dogs. The fugitives were always on the run, always looking over their shoulders. So that was where the term came from: The Land of Look-Behind.

What a terrible place to live—in a land where we are always looking back over a shoulder in fear or guilt. Only we can release this guilt—and only Christ can help us to do that through His love, forgiveness, and grace.

Even though we feel assurance from our Lord, often we are

still afraid of what lies ahead, or we still look to what lies behind. As Christians, we know that each day is a gift from God, yet the temptation to live with fear and guilt weighs heavily on our hearts.

What guilt feelings weigh heavily on your heart? Are they really worth the drain on your psychological and physical resources? Are they worth dwelling on as you allow them to separate you from God's healing presence?

Jesus told us the secret of an inner calm when he said, "Let not your hearts be troubled; believe in God, believe also in me" (John 14:1 RSV). Faith is the one key that will unlock the door of fear and guilt: faith in God's promises and faith in His power.

We do not know how heavy a load you are bearing right now. We do not know the negative parenting guilt that eats at you day and night. However, we do know what we have been through as parents of active children. And we have experienced that by the power of the Holy Spirit, anyone can endure any trial, overcome any temptation, bear up under any circumstance, and do so triumphantly.

"Lostness" and Guilt

Many parents want to let go of guilt, but do not know where to turn. Instead of feeling freedom, they suffer from "lostness." Through our work in the local church and community, we know that many parents today are in this same boat. Because they cannot deal with overwhelming feelings of guilt, they live in total lostness. Many of the most loving parents are wandering around in a moral and spiritual fog. They may be professing Christians; they may be loving and devoted mothers and fathers; they may be responsible citizens, but they have a tremendous feeling of helplessness in the face of the shifting values of our affluent and rapidly changing society.

Jesus understands. In Luke 15, we read three of Jesus' parables—about a lost sheep, a lost coin, and a lost boy. He indicated in these parables that our lostness is of grave concern to the One who created us and that there is a way in which this lostness may be found—by rediscovering and reconnecting with God.

Being Lost Is Easy

The problem is that many of us actually prefer our lostness. In our own minds, being "lost" requires less of us than being found. The idea that God really could be the personal, loving deity that the Bible describes, rejoicing like a shepherd over finding a lost sheep, rejoicing like a woman over recovering a lost coin, rejoicing like a father over seeing a lost boy come back home, is difficult to understand—when we are lost.

If we were to accept that God really is like that, think how much responsibility that would place upon us. We could not go on playing our "guilty" parenting games. Behavior changes would surely be mandated. We would have to put more time into our families instead of thinking that money can take care of time apart from our children or ignoring them after a tiring day at work. We would have to take responsibility for sharing our faith with our children and offering religious education at home as well as at church. We would have to pay more attention to our children's academic habits, encouraging and modeling good habits and setting expectations in our homes. And we would have to become godly parents. As difficult as these behaviors would be, the benefits would be substantial. As we learn to live as men and women of Christ, the result will be guilt-free living.

Moving Beyond Lostness

Is there any way out of the fog that guilt places over us? Is there a cure for our lostness? Obviously, there is, or Jesus would not have told the parables recorded in Luke 15. There can be no rejoicing shepherd, no rejoicing woman, no rejoicing father, if what is lost cannot be found. However, a few moments of reflection will tell us that there is a difference between a lost sheep, a lost coin, and a lost boy.

The prodigal son could not be found until *he took responsibility for his own life.* It was not until he "came to himself" and started back toward his father's house that there was hope for him. He was out there feeding the pigs, which for a Jewish boy would be the ultimate humiliation. Until he was willing to take the responsibility of leaving the pigpen, there was no hope for him. Once that decision was made, however, the essential victory was won.

You, too, can escape lostness. You can move beyond living with the negative guilt that tears at your very being by making a very important decision, and that is to *really believe* the good news.

There really is a loving God who cares deeply for us as individuals, as moms and dads. God cares what we do with our lives, how we raise our children, and what needless feelings of guilt we embrace when things don't go as we planned. You may think that faith is more complicated than that, but it isn't.

You know firsthand what Christian parents are up against in the world, but you also know that genuine spirituality requires inner renewal rather than outward conformity. This means that no matter what society's values are, you are to answer a higher calling. Because you are a Christian, this higher calling means that you are summoned "to live *in* the world, but not be *of* the world." You can experience an abundant life right where you are without giving in to society's secular demands. How are you to do this?

1. Know that God understands your feelings and has a plan for your life. No matter how exasperating the day is or how unruly your kids are, know that God is there. He feels your pain and sorrow. The psalmist affirms that God knows your grief: "You have seen me tossing and turning through the night. You have collected all my tears and preserved them in your bottle! You have recorded every one in your book" (Ps. 56:8 TLB).

God also sees when you act in ways that honor Him, when you uphold Christian standards of living in your home—no matter how rough it is. Zephaniah 3:17 celebrates this rejoicing, saying: "He will rejoice over you in great gladness; he will love you and not accuse you. Is that a joyous choir I hear? No, it is the Lord himself exalting over you in happy song" (TLB).

As a Christian, you do not always know why God places you where He does in life. You do not know why your child chooses to rebel or act defiantly. You do not understand why some people seem to have an easier time with family living than you do. But you do know that as difficult as your situation may be, God is with you and has a plan for you. Knowing this enables you to relax and enjoy the special joys of the moment.

2. See each day as an opportunity to share God's love. No matter what pressures you are under, remember that Christ's love is other-centered. Once you have yielded to the love of Christ, this is the way you will act—naturally reaching out to others. And as you respond to God's call to touch the lives of those around you, you will experience God's love in a greater manner than ever before.

Kozlov, a former Soviet criminal and eventual church leader, writes of life in a Soviet prison:

> Among the general despair, while prisoners like myself were cursing ourselves, the camp, the authorities; while we opened up our veins, or our stomachs, or hanged ourselves; the Christians (often with sentences of twenty to twenty-five years) did not despair. One could see Christ reflected in their faces. Their pure,

upright life, deep faith and devotion to God, their gentleness and their wonderful manliness, became a shining example of real life for thousands.[2]

This is authentic Christianity, whenever and wherever it appears.

As Christ-centered parents, our faith is not to be lived out just at church or before close friends. We are called to share God's grace with all people—yes, even in our homes and even when our children are "unlovely." In Matthew 5:16, we read: "In the same way, let your light shine before men, that they may see your good deeds and praise your Father in heaven" (NIV). We share God's love with our children when we "let our light shine" at home through "good deeds" or behaviors such as generosity, gentleness, patience, and forgiveness—even when we don't "feel" like it! These attributes will show our families and others that we are different, even in the midst of a personal conflict caused by unresolved guilt.

Seek Optimum Healing from Guilt

If only we were masters of our destinies! So many of us believe that if we only work hard enough, we will be successful and will never have to live with parenting guilt or feelings of failure. We believe that if only we are obedient to God and to each other, then trials in our families will not come our way. But life doesn't work this way. Although diligence and obedience are necessary for living a godly life, some things are out of our control.

Most of us feel helpless when feelings of guilt overwhelm us. That is where faith comes in. Faith is the conviction that there is One who is in control, whose nature is love. Sometimes that is a faint hope to hold onto, especially when daily fatigue and desperation tell us to give up.

When trials occur in our families that trigger negative guilt, it often seems impossible to face another day. Yet even though there are *no* guarantees that we will be insulated from the worst life has to offer, as Christians, we must know that the best in life is always more powerful than the worst. And the best can be experienced right now as we make decisions that draw us closer to the Cross.

GUILT-FREE CHALLENGES

1. Ellen talks about pursuing peace instead of pursuing Christ and how her life was changed when she turned to the Prince of Peace. This can be compared to the difference between trying and trusting. What actions are you taking to "try" to find inner peace? Examples might be having perfect attendance at church or praying before meals. Though these are excellent ways to begin finding inner peace, what changes would have to occur in your life and your family's life for you to start "trusting" the Prince of Peace for lasting security?

2. The Holy Spirit is the Father's heartbeat in our lives—the inner assurance that we are not alone. "Let not your hearts be troubled, neither let them be afraid" (John 14:27 RSV). It's distressing that so many of us are still afraid. Where do you turn when your guilty feelings turn to fear in your life? Write down some of the fears that haunt you each day.

3. The Bible offers great solace to the weary. What favorite verses offer you consolation during times of adversity? Write them down on sticky notes and affix them to your refrigerator, bathroom mirror, car dashboard, and other places where you will see them every day. Share these verses with your children as you teach inner strength and share your personal relationship with the One who never leaves us alone.

4. We have experienced that spiritual unrest or the search for inner peace is the unconscious motivator for seeking completeness in life. Viktor Frankl has pointed out that

this emotional unrest or inner tension is an indispensable prerequisite of mental health. That is, when we experience inner tension, we become motivated not to settle for physical comforts but to seek a more whole and complete condition. What changes would have to take place in your life for you to feel complete? You may need to have more alone time or to work part-time instead of full-time so that you can spend more time with your children. How difficult would it be to make these changes?

5. When we respond to God's call and recognize the inner spirit, the soul, we begin to embrace the true character of the being—the very essence of who we are—and we are able to tackle life's demands, including parenting, with greater enthusiasm and without the baggage of negative guilt. Make plans to revitalize your inner spirit today with a renewed commitment to a devotional life, including prayer, Bible study, and time for listening to God. Block out your devotional time on a calendar for the next month. This will help you to cultivate a devotional life.

Chapter 5

Accept Your Limitations

*A*s you are starting to realize, guilt-free parenting is about accepting yourself—weaknesses and all—and with God's help, learning to be the best you can be—right where you are in life.

However, you may be wondering if recognizing your limitations just may be another way of acknowledging low self-esteem. Hardly! It is your way of accepting a truth—that you can't do everything—and through this acceptance, you are freed to become all God intended. After all, it is part of God's plan to use your talents and gifts for His purpose.

Because we have learned to recognize our limitations, life has been much less stressful. For instance, Debra sings soprano in the church choir, but she knows that singing a solo is not for her. Similarly, Ellen enjoys sharing her testimony, but she draws the line when it comes to accepting a Bible teaching position.

But what about parenting? How does recognizing our limitations reduce the negative guilt we feel? Our friend Kate learned the hard way to identify her personal limitations. She left her full-time job with an accounting firm to stay home with her three elementary-age children, saying that workplace stress became more than she could handle. But lately, she tells of considering going back to work—because of the same feelings of stress:

> The first month I was home, life was wonderful. I was able to clean the house, organize our lives, and have dinner ready when Kenny got home. Being home when the kids got off the school bus was a special treat, and I felt good about this.
>
> Then I got bored during the day and decided to volunteer. First, it was at church two mornings a week, helping with the preschool program. Then I added another day helping in the library at the kids' school. I was offered the job of president of the school's advisory board and could not turn this down. However, after one year of staying home, I was never home. If I wasn't volunteering or leading a committee, I was picking up neighborhood kids for after-school activities. This was not in my plan at all! My stress level far exceeded that of being at work, and I began to long for those days at the office when I could close my door to the world.

Kate has realized that she needs to set strong limits in her life or she becomes full of anxiety and tension.

Love Thy Neighbor as Thyself

If you gain nothing else from this book, the most important truth we want you to understand is that you cheat your spouse, your children, your employer or coworkers, and yourself when you ignore your own needs. Recognizing your limitations will help you to draw the line between self-care and other-care, and everyone will benefit.

"But what about the scripture in the fourth chapter of Philippians that says I can do all things through Christ who strengthens me?" you might ask. Janet, an enthusiastic young woman, was not convinced that setting limits was important in her life. She continued to work full-time while raising children, volunteering in the community, and coaching her daughter's soccer team—until one day when her daughter chose not to commit to soccer for the upcoming year. Janet explained:

> Overnight, I went from volunteering nearly every night of the week to being home each night, and I had all of this time on my hands. At first, I didn't know what to do with evenings at home and weekends free. But then I realized that I had missed out on truly knowing who I was—as a person—not as a mom or wife. I started taking some art classes with my two daughters, and we thrived on this bonding time together.

Whereas Philippians 4:13 empowers us to take on life's struggles when we feel immobile, Romans 12:3 reminds us to take into account our personal limitations. Paul says, "Don't cherish exaggerated ideas of yourself or of your importance, but try to have a sane estimate of your capabilities" (Phillips). Yes, leaning on God's strength is necessary for facing life's hardships. We also must remind ourselves that, as human beings, we do have limits.

In Mark 12:31, we find the second part of the Great Commandment: "You shall love your neighbor as yourself" (RSV). This verse presupposes that we love ourselves. However, as we have experienced personally, if we are full of tensions, anxieties, and exhaustion, perhaps we are not loving ourselves enough. As many have learned the hard way, unless we draw limits in our lives and truly care for ourselves, we may not be equipped to love and care for others.

Discover Your Comfort Zone

One helpful way to draw limits in your life is to identify your God-given gifts. Paul suggested to the Romans that they identify and use their gifts. We suggest you do this as well, beginning with the Personal Worksheet on page 88. First, identify your talents and write them in the Comfort Zone. List the very things that you enjoy doing, the actions that come easily to you. On the opposite side, list your limitations. These are the things that do not come easily—actions that cause you stress or that are stumbling blocks in your daily living. A sample worksheet is provided on page 87 as an example.

As children of God, we are made in this image. We also are given specific gifts and talents to use on God's earth. Learning what your talents *are* and what they *are not* ... will help tremendously as you pursue your goal to live guilt-free as a parent.

Sample Worksheet

Comfort Zone	*Uncomfortable Zone*
1. Cooking	1. Housekeeping
2. Working with computers	2. Doing personal finances
3. Conducting a Bible study	3. Teaching Sunday school
4. Singing in the choir	4. Playing the piano
5. Gardening	5. Decorating
6. Being a good listener	6. Making speeches to groups
7. Enjoying children	7. Being in large groups
8. Spending time with friends	8. Attending formal gatherings
9. Sewing clothes	9. Making crafts
10. Thinking	10. Writing

Personal Worksheet

Comfort Zone	*Uncomfortable Zone*
1.	1.
2.	2.
3.	3.
4.	4.
5.	5.
6.	6.
7.	7.
8.	8.
9.	9.
10.	10.

Now that you have completed your lists, go back and review them. Are you living mostly in your Comfort Zone or in your Uncomfortable Zone? If you are living mostly in your Comfort Zone, you probably have successfully identified your talents along with your limitations, and you have learned to use them in the right ways to make your life less stressful or guilt-free. However, if you find that most of the things you do fall in your Uncomfortable Zone, then you need to acknowledge your limitations, reevaluate your commitments, and learn to make choices and delegate to others.

No matter how many cookbooks she reads, Debra admits that recipes with more than four ingredients just don't turn out for her. Accepting that cooking gourmet meals is not in her Comfort Zone, she chooses to prepare simple but nutritious meals and spend more time developing her talents, such as writing, singing, or teaching her children. Robert says that having to do the family finances falls into his Uncomfortable Zone, so he turns this job over to Debra, who admits that this is in her Comfort Zone. Instead, Robert enjoys doing the laundry or yard work and gardening.

In Ellen's home, she finds that home maintenance is definitely not in her Comfort Zone; her husband, John, however, not only enjoys it but also is very talented at it. That, in turn, allows Ellen more time to be creative in the kitchen. John builds patios and fixes leaks while Ellen prepares delicious meals.

We encourage you to lean toward your Comfort Zone as you make commitments at home and elsewhere; acknowledging that you have limitations can be a most exhilarating experience. Please note, however, that having something in your Uncomfortable Zone does not mean that you can avoid doing it from time to time. You may be called to use these very weaknesses to help those around you.

One of Aesop's fables tells of a handsome buck who came to

a spring to drink. He caught a glimpse of his reflection in the water and admired his strong and beautifully shaped antlers. He was not as impressed with the appearance of his legs. They looked so thin and weak.

While the buck was engrossed in admiring himself in the spring, a lion appeared and charged toward him. The buck fled and easily outdistanced the lion, for his true strength was in his legs. In the open fields, he had no problem staying in front of the lion.

Unfortunately, he soon ran into wooded country, where his antlers became entangled in the branches of a tree. The lion caught him. The buck thought to himself, "Alas! My legs, which I thought were too frail, were my salvation. My antlers, which I thought to be my strength, were my destruction."

There are times when we have to push ourselves a bit harder to get through the day. Even though we may hate doing house-work, getting up for work each day, or mowing the yard, we know we must do it anyway. Remember that God can use any-thing we offer to Him in a great and wondrous way. Each of us has something to offer God and to offer the family, no matter how small it may seem.

As children of God, we are made in His image. We also are given specific gifts and talents to use on God's earth. Learning what your talents *are* and what they *are not* may take some time, but it will help tremendously as you pursue your goal to live guilt-free as a parent.

Dispel Guilty-Parenting Myths

As you begin to distinguish between your gifts and your limi-tations, you can work toward dispelling parenting myths. Robert and Debra, for example, eliminated the guilty-parenting myth that both parents must tuck the children in at night. When their children were young, Robert, who enjoyed staying up late at night, would put the three to bed and say bedtime prayers while Debra went to bed early. She would then awaken before the children, make breakfast and school lunches, and have a morning devotion with the children before school while Robert slept in.

To decrease negative parenting guilt, find what works for your family and feel comfortable in doing just that. Remember what we talked about in chapter 1, that your family is given permission to write its own script. You can choose what works best for you without comparing this to any other family. God brought you together as a unique entity, each with his or her own Comfort Zone. Celebrate this uniqueness by finding what works in *your* home. Learn to help others in your family with their limitations as you lean on your strengths and get through the day—without guilt.

As you think more about what will work in your home, consider the following guilty-parenting myths and the actual guilt-free facts:

1. Guilty-Parenting Myth: As a parent, I must be on call every minute of the day for my family.

Guilt-Free Fact: While your family is extremely important in your life, you owe yourself time during the day to focus on your interests and well-being. This means taking a nap (even if only fifteen minutes), going on a stress-reduction walk, or reading a book that you enjoy—without feeling guilty. No one will tell you to do any of this; in fact, it is our experience that we must watch out for ourselves when it comes to personal priorities and self-care.

2. Guilty-Parenting Myth: Even if I'm tired after working full-time and parenting my three children, I owe it to my family to have a hot meal and a spotless home.

Guilt-Free Fact: Everyone gets tired. On days when you feel you have little left to give, order out. Call for pizza and complement it with a salad or fresh fruit and skim milk. Have a race to see who can pick up the most clutter in the house, and toss an afghan over the pile of dirty clothes. Always remember that tomorrow is another day.

3. Guilty-Parenting Myth: I should feel happy that my children want to talk with me each night, but sometimes I get distracted and need peace.

Guilt-Free Fact: The needs of your children are endless, but your personal needs are important, too. Take time each day to talk with them, but also allow yourself time to be alone—to have quiet time or to play peaceful music while all family members read. You might consider a "Day Is Done" time when you and your spouse go to your room to read or talk, and the children do the same.

4. Guilty-Parenting Myth: As a single parent, I just went back to work. I should be able to handle this, along with caring for my two preschoolers at night, but I am in overload.

Guilt-Free Fact: Caring for children is a difficult job in itself, much less combining their care with the stress of working outside the home. Use the tips in this book to prioritize your life, set goals that are important for you and your children, and take time out during the day to renew your strength—even if only for a few minutes—so you can get through the busy nights as a "good enough" parent. Chapter 6 has some practical suggestions that all parents can use to reduce their level of stress and avoid burnout.

5. Guilty-Parenting Myth: My kids have enough pressure just trying to make good grades at school and participate in sports activities without asking them to have home responsibilities.

Guilt-Free Fact: Why hinder their development? Allowing your children the *privilege* of doing household responsibilities is a perk for them. Not only do they feel a vital part of the family, but they also learn skills that will be useful when they reach adulthood. They will need to know how to wash clothes, stay on a budget, and mop floors when they leave for college or career. Remember, age is on their side; they have more energy than you do. Share the load so that everyone enjoys life—including you!

6. Guilty-Parenting Myth: As a mother, I should be responsible for the emotional support of my child.

Guilt-Free Fact: Both parents should bond emotionally with the child. Fathers can offer words of comfort and support just as mothers can. In a time when both mothers and fathers share home responsibilities and earn income for the family, both also should be totally involved in the child's life.

These are just a few of the many guilty-parenting myths that can plague us. If you want to dispel them completely, find what works in your home. Then continually remind yourself that you are *one* person.

Remember That You Are One Person

No matter how responsible you feel, you cannot continue to play the role of Super Dad or Wonder Mom without living with feelings of exhaustion and stress. We have been there, and we know that life is too short to live on a racing roller coaster with no hope of stopping. It's time to put on the brakes!

Kerri, a single parent, shared this about working full-time when her daughter was a preschooler:

> After getting up at 5:00 A.M. to make breakfasts, bag lunches, do the laundry, and then get Whitney to preschool before work, I could hardly crawl in bed at night. Whitney, who napped all afternoon at day care, was always full of energy during the evening. I knew that reading stories to her was important, but I had to do what was right for both of us.
>
> One Saturday, I taped her favorite stories, nursery rhymes, and music. At the end of the tape, I recorded some prayers and simple scripture verses. Now at 8:00 P.M. each night, I read Whitney her bedtime story and we say our prayers. Then as she starts to beg for more and more stories, I turn the tape on beside her bed. She listens contentedly and drifts to sleep; I get to crawl in bed with a smile on my face and not feel guilty that I am ignoring her.

Say this aloud: "I am only one." When the pressure cooker of life begins to explode, remember that you are one person. Taking on the responsibilities of just one person is what busy, guilt-free parents must do. We can do the best possible or be "good enough," but we also have to recognize our humanness and allow for this.

Compensate for Your Limitations

What limitations are you faced with each day? As you will learn in chapter 7, setting priorities is essential. Making daily "to do" lists is helpful, for we do the very things that are a priority for us. It is also important to know when negative feelings are engulfing us so that we may stop the chain of events before we explode.

In an informal interview, we asked parents what their personal limitations were, and these were some of the responses:

* I *hate* doing the family bills each month. I get so *anxious* when we don't stay within our budget.

* I get *tired* easily after working full-time and parenting teenagers.

* I *don't enjoy* staying at home full-time raising my two preschoolers. I daydream about going back to teaching.

* My husband travels, and I love people. I get *depressed* when I don't get to talk to any adults during the week.

* I *dislike* having to clean the entire house, even though I do like to stay home with my toddler.

* My baby won't sleep through the night, so I'm *tired* and *irritable* all the time.

The list of personal limitations goes on and on, but no matter what the limitation may be, there is a solution that can work—if you start to understand the limitation and take action to compensate for it.

For example, if you get irritable easily because of a child who wakes up at night, plan to take a nap during the day, and don't let anyone interfere with this time-out. Take the phone off the hook, put a "Do Not Disturb" sign on the front door, and let this nap time be your daily ritual. Even if your child does not nap, perhaps he can learn to stay in his room and read or play while you get your much-needed rest. If you work outside the home, find a way to set aside a few minutes before or after dinner for the necessity of rest.

Annie told us that she requires a lot of sleep to cope with her busy life. When her youngest child was born, she had a difficult time functioning on less sleep than her body needed. "Trying to feed the baby every four hours, along with taking care of an active three-year-old, was overwhelming," she said. "I finally decided that I could feed the baby at 8:00 P.M., then go to bed when my preschooler did. My husband would feed the baby at midnight before he went to bed, then I would wake up at 4:00 A.M. for the early morning feeding, while my husband could sleep until 7:30 A.M." After Annie recognized her limitation of needing a good night's sleep, she was able to compensate for it, and everyone's life was smoother.

Perhaps you struggle with feelings of resentment because your spouse's career seems more glamorous than chasing a toddler. Make plans with other parents in your neighborhood to go out together several times a week. Consider joining a Bible study group at your church. Or take an aerobics class at the YMCA where child care is provided. Meet at a nearby park for "adult" talk while the children enjoy the outdoors. Staying home with children does not mean staying lonely, and it should not be done out of guilt!

Or perhaps you become easily stressed from life's interruptions. Learn to monitor your commitments using the information in chapter 7, and make only those obligations that you can easily keep while raising children. The point is this: You *can* find ways to compensate for any limitation you may have.

To illustrate this further, let us explore in more detail two of the most common limitations of parents: lack of sleep and insufficient time alone.

Get Plenty of Sleep

"Sure, I'd get plenty of sleep if only I had a chance," said Mindy, the mother of a toddler and a newborn. "As soon as I get in bed, I fall asleep, only to awaken again within a few hours to feed the baby. I run on low fuel all the time because of a sleep deficit. Then because I'm tired, I'm irritable with my husband and children, which adds to my guilt."

Millions of people suffer from sleep deprivation, especially busy parents who are trying to balance kids, careers, and community involvement. One study found that Americans have cut their sleep time by 20 percent in the last century. This reduction of sleep time is a problem for the majority of adults, who need at least seven hours of sleep each night. Adults who slept only six hours each night experienced more frequent health problems, and over a period of nine years these "shorter sleepers" had a 70 percent higher mortality rate.

Anything that influences our bodies also affects our minds. Disrupted sleep not only affects how we feel physically, but it also can create a weakened emotional state. Studies show that severe sleep deprivation can even lead to psychotic episodes.

Most of us know the importance of sleep to our physical and mental health, yet it is not always easy to get a good night's sleep. Whereas most children and teens sleep almost 100 percent of the time they spend in bed, as we move into our late thirties and beyond, sleep problems become a reality. Beyond age thirty-five, the efficiency of our sleep decreases as we spend less and less time in bed actually sleeping. Why is this?

Studies indicate that the production of melatonin—a brain hormone produced by the pineal gland—decreases as we age. Scientists have long recognized that melatonin is a key factor in the body's biological clock. The production of melatonin stops each morning as the body receives wake-up signals. Then in the evening as the body receives signals that the day is ending, such as darkness and quiet, the production of melatonin resumes, making us sleepy. When we remain in loud, bright, active environments prior to bedtime or when thoughts of our responsibilities keep our minds running on "red alert," the production of melatonin is interrupted, and we have difficulty falling asleep. Naturally, when we produce lower levels of melatonin as we age, we often find it even more challenging to get a good night's rest.

If you have difficulty sleeping because of too much job stress or parenting-related anxieties, try the following helpful suggestions:

* Sleep only as much as you need to feel refreshed, but no more. Some people lose sleep all week, then try to make up for the loss on the weekend. This only disrupts the body's circadian rhythm. Circadian rhythms are separate, individually synchronized internal rhythms that affect our daily sleep cycles, performance and alertness, moods, and even gastrointestinal function.

* Wake up at the same time every day, including weekends. Having a regular wake-up time strengthens your circadian cycle and helps to establish regular sleep patterns.

* Use earplugs or "white noise" if you are bothered by noises while sleeping. White noise—a humming sound or static noise—is also helpful to those who have difficulty sleeping in complete silence. You can purchase a noise machine that produces white noise or tune your radio "between stations" for a similar effect.

* Eat a snack high in serotonin-boosting carbohydrates to lull you to dreamland. Some crackers or a bagel might relax you. Don't allow hunger to disrupt your sleep.

* Avoid caffeine after noon each day. Caffeine disturbs sound sleep.

* Avoid alcohol. While some may think that alcohol helps

them to sleep, it actually produces a light, fragmented sleep.

* Exercise regularly. But avoid exercise late in the day because it might stimulate you and make falling asleep difficult.

* Avoid daytime napping if you have trouble sleeping at night. If you need to rest, sit up in a chair and listen to music or read a book. Naps can prevent sound sleep at nighttime.

Take Time for Yourself

Another common limitation of parents is insufficient "quiet time" for themselves. Contrary to what some believe, planning your daily schedule so that you have time alone does not mean turning your back on your children or spouse when they need you most. After all, as Christians, we believe that human souls are eternal, and whatever touches the lives of your family members has eternal significance. A helpful question to ask yourself is, What difference will this make or how important will it be in five years? For example, if your daughter needs to talk about a problem she is having at school and you are just sitting down to read a good book, do what is eternal—talk with your child. The book can wait. Nevertheless, it is possible to take time for yourself without neglecting your family.

There is a time for silence; unfortunately, most of us don't experience this often enough. Many of us live for that moment each night when we can close the bedroom door and shut out the problems of the day. Especially if we are meeting the unending demands of children along with a busy career, being alone allows us to replenish the strength and renewal necessary to cope with problems. How can we hear God's voice when we drown Him out in the cacophony of noises with which we surround ourselves daily?

The Bible has a wealth of insight into the need to be alone. Being alone, as indicated by the life of Jesus, need not be a time for feeling sorry for yourself. It can be a time for finding meaning in your life. When Jesus was in solitude, He found His source of power. After spending the day preaching to and teaching the vast crowds, He went up to a mountain by Himself to pray (Matt.14:23). Luke told how Jesus spent time teaching and nurturing the people, then He "withdrew to the wilderness and prayed" (Luke 5:16 RSV).

At the beginning of the week, plan time each day to be alone. It could be time each evening after your spouse and children are in bed or time in the early morning before your family arises. Ellen and Debra find that early morning time is sacred, allowing them to be alone with God through prayer and study as well as to set daily goals. Robert admits to being a night owl, staying up after the family goes to bed so that he can be alone with God and his thoughts. His quiet time allows him to reflect on the day's happenings and to chart new goals for the next day.

Whatever time you set aside, use this quiet time to reflect on

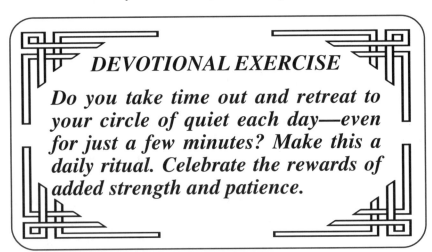

DEVOTIONAL EXERCISE

Do you take time out and retreat to your circle of quiet each day—even for just a few minutes? Make this a daily ritual. Celebrate the rewards of added strength and patience.

the past day or week and sort through the busyness of your schedule. Let this private time be a source of spiritual strength as you communicate with God, read scriptures for inspiration, and listen to God's voice in response. You will benefit greatly from this time as you unclutter your thoughts and focus on what is important.

Move On and Celebrate Life

King David's prayer, as shared in the Psalms, can be repeated by all when parenting guilt becomes obsessive and only God can lift this burden. He writes,

> Have mercy on me, O God,
> according to your unfailing love. . . .
> Cleanse me . . . , and I will be clean;
> wash me, and I will be whiter than snow. (Ps. 51:1, 7 NIV)

How quick we are to blame our shortcomings on our weaknesses! Using the information in this chapter, we want you to learn to celebrate life by acknowledging that you do have weaknesses, then rejoice in the very gifts you have. Take care of yourself as a person (see "Your Parenting Rights" on pages 102-03), remember that you are not perfect, let go of the guilt, and move on with life. You can use the organizational tools in chapter 7 to refocus your life, set new goals, and address your family's priorities.

Preoccupation with the many responsibilities of parenting can cause a tremendous amount of distracting mental activity that can hinder productive communication and lead to parenting burnout. If you feel overwhelmed with the stress of parenting, you may find it helpful or necessary to seek psychological intervention in order to develop effective communication strategies to deal with your life. As we explain in the next chapter, burnout is one aspect of guilty parenting that must be solved, and we will show you how!

Your Parenting Rights

You have rights as a parent. However, only you can stand up for yourself and these rights. When you do, you take a giant step toward guilt-free parenting.

You have the right to:

1. Take care of yourself, for this will help you take better care of your child and others. Eat right, get adequate rest, take time out, and sometimes say "no" to family and friends. (Remember to weigh the "eternal significance" of your decision. See page 99.)

2. Seek help from others. Call your pastor, doctor, or other professional if you have a concern that is creating havoc in your family.

3. Maintain your own interests and life, including paying attention to career and personal needs.

4. Get angry and express your feelings in an appropriate manner. Don't forget that you are the family's manager. Set the home rules, and expect your children to follow them.

5. Reject attempts by your child to manipulate you through anger or peer pressure. Be a "united front" with your spouse as you hold strong to rules.

6. Receive respect, forgiveness, affection, and acceptance. These attributes are expected in functional families, and you have the duty to teach your child how to treat you justly.

7. Offer respect, forgiveness, affection, and acceptance. The best way for a child to learn these attributes is for you to role model them.

8. Take pride in your accomplishments, and applaud the courage it takes to meet the many demands of life. If your life is in balance, stand proud!

9. Maintain a full personal life so that when your child grows up and leaves home, you will not be lost. Cultivate your marriage and hobbies so that your later days will be fulfilling.

10. Stay involved in church and attend regularly. Make spiritual nourishment important to your family so that you have a source of strength when facing life's interruptions.

GUILT-FREE CHALLENGES

1. What are your personal limitations? Do you acknowledge them openly, or do you struggle daily to compensate by giving and doing more than is necessary? Acknowledging your limitations will help you to reduce the negative guilt you feel as you call on others to help compensate for them.

2. Identify your Comfort Zone and your Uncomfortable Zone using the worksheets on pages 87 and 88. Is your Comfort Zone or Uncomfortable Zone longer? Are you comfortable in letting others use their talents in those uncomfortable areas of your life? Are you giving more to others in your Comfort Zone? If so, talk openly with your family about every member contributing to make one whole. Explain the importance of everyone in the family pulling his or her weight.

3. It is difficult to accept the fact that we can do only so much in life. However, no matter how responsible you feel, it is necessary to realize that you are one person. What are some ways you can take time out during your busy day, without anyone else around, to celebrate your existence as a child of God?

4. Affirming our own needs does not mean ignoring others. As Christians, we know that human souls are eternal, and we are accountable for touching lives with the love of God. Spend some quality time today with your spouse and

with each child. Affirm their Comfort Zones, and help them to accept their Uncomfortable Zones.

5. Are sleep problems affecting your ability to be a "guilt-free" parent? If so, reread the suggestions on pages 98-99 and follow them for sounder sleep.

Chapter 6

Prevent Parenting Burnout

*M*ost would agree that it is virtually impossible to be all things to all people and live without needless guilt. It is hard to be a perfect wife, loving mother, caring daughter, ambitious employee, dedicated volunteer, and compassionate friend without losing something—usually your physical, emotional, or spiritual health. Why, then, do so many busy parents feel guilty if they are not continually providing for their children? They are simply unable to put aside time for themselves to recharge their batteries. This lack of personal caring results in a powerful state: burnout.

Instead of falling apart when burnout is approaching, we believe that parents can use this state as a firm reminder to take time for themselves and strike a balance between their own needs and those of their family.

You've heard the question before: What would you save from your house or apartment if it was on fire and you could make only one trip back in? Responses to the question seem to differ

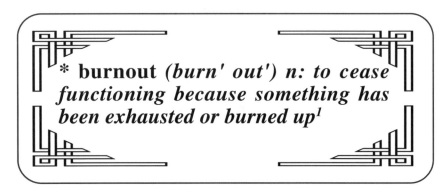

** **burnout** (burn' out') n: to cease functioning because something has been exhausted or burned up[1]*

depending on age, stage of life, and background. Nevertheless, some common responses include photo albums, baby books, and home videos. These individuals want to make sure their family history and memories are preserved for the next generations.

Likewise, responses to this chapter will vary. For some of you, this chapter may very well be your redeeming chance to run back in and save yourself because you are on the verge of physical, emotional, and even spiritual burnout. For others, this chapter can help you change the batteries in your smoke alarm before the fire engines are called in. In either case, this chapter will help you recognize the signs of burnout and learn how to prevent a "fire" from destroying your home.

Understanding the Stress Factor

Listed below are some definitions of the words *burn* and *out*. Look over the lists and check any that identify your personal feelings.

Burn

____ To undergo rapid combustion
____ To feel heat or a physiologically similar sensation
____ To give off heat

_____ To produce pain or a stinging sensation similar to that of fire

_____ To feel extreme anger

_____ To feel strong emotion

_____ To become charred or overcooked by heat

_____ To be damned

_____ To suffer losses

Out

_____ Away from, not in, the normal, usual place or state

_____ To a state of exhaustion, extinction, or depletion

_____ Out of joint; in or into a state of confusion

_____ In a direction away from center or inside

_____ Beyond possession, control, or occupation

_____ To become publicly known

If you have not examined your life and all your activities recently, we want you to stop and take an honest assessment. If you checked *any* of the definitions of the words *burn* and *out*, you are demonstrating signs of stress.

Stress is a biological phenomenon that affects the central nervous system, autonomic nervous system, and the endocrine and immune systems. It is a key contributing factor to illness, including

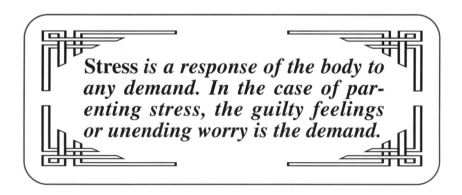

Stress *is a response of the body to any demand. In the case of parenting stress, the guilty feelings or unending worry is the demand.*

heart disease, depression, anxiety disorders, asthma, allergy, and cancer. As guilt bears on your heart and soul day after day, month after month, the body begins to react to this constant stressor.

We experience stress as the fight-or-flight reaction to external or internal pressures, which is our natural instinct to fight or flee from danger. The problem arises when we experience this fight-or-flight response on a daily basis, which can occur when we feel angry, pressured, frustrated, or guilty. Even though we may not acknowledge that we are under stress, there is still an increased flow of adrenaline into the body, which increases heart rate, blood pressure, and muscle tension. The increase in adrenaline is the way that we prepare ourselves to either fight the perceived danger or flee it. When the stressful event is over, the body soon recovers, and all body systems return to normal. However, when this stress response persists day after day with no release, chronic functional changes may lead to physical or emotional illness.

The important word to note is *response*. Whatever the stressor may be, it represents only 10 percent of the problem; the other 90 percent is the response to it. In other words, the danger lies not in the stressor itself but in the personal reaction.

When you are overworked or overcommitted, feelings of negative guilt can escalate, putting you into *reactive gear.* When you are in reactive gear, you allow your feelings to drive you, without thinking about how you want to express them. Not only does reactive gear make you feel vulnerable, but it also can negatively affect your relationships at home and on the job.

After noting the warning signs of stress listed here, take a moment to think about how your body responds to unending guilt. Which signs of stress have been evident in your life? What others have you experienced? Knowing you have your own specific stress reaction to guilt, you can learn to listen to your body before the stress immobilizes you.

Warning Signs of Stress

* Anger
* Anxiety
* Back pain
* Body aches and pains
* Boredom
* Bossiness
* Bowel or bladder changes
* Compulsive eating
* Compulsive gum chewing
* Constant worrying
* Crying
* Dizziness
* Dry mouth
* Edginess
* Excessive smoking
* Easily upset
* Feeling immobilized
* Forgetfulness
* Headaches and other aches
* Inability to make decisions
* Indigestion
* Lack of creativity
* Lightheadedness
* Loneliness
* Loss of sense of humor
* Memory loss
* Nervousness
* Palpitations
* Racing heart
* Restlessness
* Ringing in ears
* Sleep disturbances
* Sweaty palms
* Unhappiness

The Sinkhole Syndrome

Stress is nothing new, and much has been written about it. In his book *Ordering Your Private World*, Gordon MacDonald appropriately refers to "stress" and "burnout" as the Sinkhole Syndrome. He writes, "Sinkholes occur when underground streams drain away during seasons of drought, causing the ground at the surface to lose its underlying support. Suddenly, everything simply caves in, leaving people with a frightening suspicion that nothing—not even the earth beneath their feet—is trustworthy."[2] MacDonald goes on to say that there are many people whose lives are on the verge of a cave-in due to fatigue, feelings of failure, or disillusionment about goals or purpose. Often we feel that we are just a step away from going under. What is wrong? The Sinkhole, formed by burnout, can result from a multitude of causes, but often there is a hidden and deeply rooted cause brought about by either circumstance or environment. Guilt is once again the culprit.

As we have experienced, guilt-motivated parents are tired parents. Some "break" quickly. Others can wear the mask for years until they cross the line into burnout. Mothers seem to wear the mask longer and make especially good martyrs. Debra and Ellen confess to falling into this trap several times over their parenting years.

Guilt drives us to do more and more. MacDonald reports that many people are driven toward goals and objectives without always understanding why, and without understanding what they are doing to their minds, bodies, hearts—and we might add, their families. Driven people are not necessarily "bad" people. They often start organizations, make significant contributions, and offer ways and means of doing things that benefit other people. But drivenness, as we discussed in chapter 4, is not the way to lasting peace and guilt-free living.

Read the following statements defining driven people adapted from McDonald's book, and see if you recognize any of the same tendencies in your own life—or perhaps in the life of your spouse:

1. Driven people are most often gratified only by accomplishment.

A person begins to reason that if one accomplishment resulted in good feelings and the praise of others, then several more accomplishments will bring an abundance of good feeling and affirmations. Children who are taught they must always perform, or who are constantly praised, have a tendency to become driven adults.

2. Driven people are preoccupied with the symbols of accomplishment.

They are generally concerned with their own notoriety and are aware of status symbols, such as titles, office size and location, positions or organizational charts, and special privileges. They keep up with the Joneses at work and at home, at all costs.

3. Driven people are usually caught up in the pursuit of expansion.

They like to be part of something that is getting bigger and more successful and rarely have any time to appreciate the achievements to date. They teach their children that enough is never enough.

4. Driven people tend to have a limited regard for integrity.

They become so preoccupied with success and achievement that they have little time to stop and assess their own emotional state. People like this often become deceitful, deceiving others as well as themselves.

5. Driven people often possess limited or undeveloped people skills.

Projects become more important than people. If others are not found to be helpful, they are disregarded. This includes families and children.

6. Driven people tend to be highly competitive.

Driven persons feel they must win. Winning provides them with much needed self-worth. Their children are not acceptable if they are not always the best.

7. Driven people have a tendency toward eruptive anger.

Anger can be triggered when anyone disagrees or offers a different plan or solution. Angry parents model this behavior for their children. The inability to handle conflict and anger destroys homes and marriages.

8. Driven people are often abnormally busy.

They are usually too busy for ordinary relationships with spouse, family, or friends. They rarely think they have accomplished enough, so they seize every available minute to attend more meetings, lead more groups, and volunteer for more activities. Busyness becomes a way of life. They find it enjoyable to complain and gather pity for all they do.[3]

Murphy's Law

Whether we are rich or poor, whether we work outside the home or are stay-at-home parents, all of us are susceptible to letting our guilt drive us. Lisa's story could be the testimony of many.

Lisa and her husband, Kevin, worked hard to have a nice income and house before they had children. Lisa insisted that everything be perfect. Her dad had said that she would never amount to much, and that had been an underlying driving force in her life. Lisa and Kevin made sure they got their names on a waiting list with the top day care in the area, even before their first baby was born. When their first child was two, they began trying to have another child and conceived immediately. Six weeks after baby number two was born, Lisa once again returned to the office, putting both girls in day care.

All seemed to be working as planned until Kevin was promoted to another position that required more travel. Suddenly, it was all Lisa could do to get both girls to day care and herself to work when Kevin was out a week at a time. When he was gone over a weekend, Lisa had no opportunity to regroup before the next week. After several months, Lisa and Kevin made the very difficult decision for her to quit work. They sold their house and scaled down to a smaller place where they were comfortable, yet a little cramped.

It took Lisa a good while to settle in to motherhood from eight to five, but when she finally did, she began to experience some relief from the stress that had ruled her life for all those months. She was determined not to put her girls in Mother's Day Out or even a part-time preschool program. She even thought about home schooling them. She was going to be a full-time, devoted mother. She started leading church activities and enrolled the girls in ballet and acrobatics. She volunteered at a Senior Adult Center two times a week and took the girls with her. And then the unexpected happened.

Kevin's mother, a widow, was diagnosed with cancer. Kevin was an only child and lived two states away, so the only solution was for Grandma to move in with Kevin, Lisa, and the girls.

Lisa moved the girls into one room and set up the extra room with a hospital bed for Grandma. When Kevin traveled, Lisa cared for both girls and his mother. She wanted the girls' lives to continue as usual, but they couldn't afford sitters for Kevin's mother very often. Lisa tried to continue some of her church responsibilities, but she could not attend regularly.

When Kevin's mother died, Lisa was completely depleted. She looked ten years older and had dropped out of everything, including church. Lisa did not understand that life is not about perfection. The unexpected always happens. We even have a name for it—Murphy's Law. And whoever Murphy is, he shows up when we least expect it. He is no respecter of persons. Life is more about how we handle the unexpected. It's the old "you can make lemonade from lemons" philosophy. Knowing we are going to face some difficult challenges in life, then it makes good sense to stay in control of the stressful drive that guilt can produce.

Lisa was in trouble from the very beginning of her marriage. Her obsession with creating a perfect family could never last. Her "support" or motivation was wrapped up in her busyness. When the unexpected happened and that support caved in, even though she had done some very good things, Lisa's activities could not keep her world from crumbling.

Prevention Intervention

So how do you keep from ending up like Lisa? First, if you recognize yourself in any of the burnout, stress, or driven persons descriptions, *stop and seek help.* Talk to your spouse, a trusted friend, or a Christian counselor or minister. Get a "reading" on your guilt. This does not indicate that you are weak or that you are not depending on God enough. It indicates that you are concerned enough about the you God created to make sure you are experiencing God's best for yourself and your family. It demonstrates good stewardship of what God has given you.

To guard against parenting burnout, consider some of these suggestions.

1. Consider involvement in only one thing.

Allow your children to choose one interest at a time and agree on how long they will be involved. Think through how you spend your time and see if you can trim back and attempt only one of some things:

One activity
One project
One trip
One class
One ministry

You may even want to give special attention to each child one day a week or allow each family member to be honored one week a month. That way each child can feel special without having to share the spotlight with another sibling. And you can give quality attention to each child without having to spread yourself so thin every day.

2. Share the load.

Your spouse and children will not know that you need them to share the load unless you communicate that to them and teach them how to work together as a family unit. Consider a family helper chart. Assign or allow each family member to choose a chore for a day or a week, such as doing the laundry. Believe it or not, it is not written anywhere that the mother should be a human laundromat! Children need to learn how to wash clothes, fold them, and put them away. At first, you will have to help them separate the clothes properly and learn the other steps. Let them help you make a chart that gives them step-by-step instructions, and hang it near the washer and dryer. Encourage your family to work as a team.

As Ellen's children have grown, they have been given more household responsibilities and have become part of the family "team" that keeps the home front running on course. Each family member has a laundry day when he or she is expected to wash the dirty clothes, fold them, and deliver them to the appropriate rooms. Her teens also rotate responsibility for setting the table for dinner and clearing away the dishes each night. These responsibilities have helped the children understand that in a family, it takes more than just taking care of yourself; it takes a team working together.

No one person should or can do all the "dirty work." If one person constantly does all the household chores, she or he will certainly burn out quickly. We are accountable for the well-being and health of one another.

3. Be a kinder person—to yourself.

At least once a day, do something nice for yourself and your marriage. Once a week, do something especially nice for yourself and your marriage. Debra always reserves "alone time" for a devotional period or for reading favorite magazines or books. During this time, she sometimes calls close friends and family members. Robert likes to turn on relaxing music as he spends time alone during the evening hours. This helps to calm his inner drive and bring him to a more reflective state. Together, they sit outside on the patio each evening after dinner and have some alone time together. On Friday night, going out to dinner, taking a walk on the beach, or having a sunset picnic in a nearby park is a common outing—without kids.

You may want to schedule a Friday night bubble bath, complete with candles and your favorite CD. If your children are young, let your spouse or older child take care of them while you take a much-needed time-out. If you are the only one who takes care of the kids, wait until they are asleep or provide fun activities to keep them entertained for your thirty-minute quiet time (see number 4).

4. Provide fun activities for your child to occupy her during your "alone time."

Make your own sing-along and read-along tapes with accompanying "books." Your child will love hearing your voice on the tape and looking at a book you have written and put together yourself. Rotate her favorite videotapes. Let her make special pictures for you while you enjoy your alone time; then display the pictures on the refrigerator for the next week. Put old clothes and jewelry in a dress-up box. Save some of these items to use just for playtime when Mommy or Daddy needs alone time. Be creative and try different ways to make this a special time she will look forward to.

5. Once a week, enforce "Double D Time."

This means "Do" or "Don't" and offers your child a choice. He can choose to interrupt you during your alone time, or he can choose not to. Explain to your child that this is your special time when you are not to be interrupted, with a few exceptions. Then clearly define the acceptable reasons for interruptions. Make a list or draw pictures to remind your child of these acceptable reasons, so that he does not have to come and ask you. If your child interrupts you without justifiable cause, then he must suffer an appropriate consequence, such as losing some special time he values. For example, if he is allowed to watch a certain TV show or play outside after school, then he would lose that time the next day.

On the other hand, if he "Doesn't" interrupt you, you can reward him with lots of hugs and kisses. You may want to make a sign that says "Double D," or even "D D" for younger children, and hang it on your door during your "alone time." Whether he "Does" or "Doesn't," your child will get the message if you follow through with rewards or consequences.

Note: This activity is more appropriate for older preschoolers and school-age children. For younger children, start with fifteen minutes and increase by five-minute intervals as they become accustomed to the activity and as they mature. Use family time to discuss "Double D Time" options for each individual. And don't forget to unplug the phone!

6. Trade off time with a friend.

Contract with a friend to trade children once a week. One week you keep all the kids for a day; the next week, she does. Many parents have started this with one friend and later included more friends. More friends means more children, so create an easy-to-follow chart that indicates who will keep the children each week. If the group continues to grow, friends can work in pairs or in threes to keep the children. Limit your group to children around the same age, making it easier to plan snacks and activities.

7. Take advantage of getaways.

If you feel you are dangerously close to burnout, try an immediate getaway. If you can get away for a weekend, do it. If not, try it for a night or an evening. As we have said, even a thirty-minute bubble bath can make a big difference. If you schedule some getaway time at least once a week, your children will become accustomed to it.

8. Think of shortcuts that really help.

If your child is usually starving by the time you get home from work, provide a small snack for the car ride—preferably something that does not increase hyperactivity. Try dry cereal, fruit, snack crackers, animal crackers, and so forth. If the weather is warm, provide something cold to drink. Not only will this keep your child occupied as you drive, but it also will allow you to take time to relax before you must prepare supper.

Remember, anything you can do the night before is better than trying to do it all the next morning. Your child can help fix a lunch or lay out his clothes for the next day. If you don't have any energy left to physically get it together, then make a list and put it where you will see it the next morning to help you remember details.

9. Take mininaps.

Sometimes a quick nap before supper or right after supper will allow you to give more time to your child each evening. If you stay home during the day, take a nap with your child when you need it. Often, older siblings can entertain younger ones for thirty minutes while a parent naps. Children have trouble understanding time, so help them relate by setting a kitchen timer or by resting while they watch half of *Sesame Street*.

10. Drop an activity.

Preventing parenting burnout means learning when you or your children have had enough. It is far better to lose an activity than to lose the trust of your child or your health. Other people may not like your dropping out of a particular activity, but other people do not have to give the time to your family each day that you do.

11. Drop an attitude.

For seven days in a row, evaluate what upsets you. Stress causes you to look for the negative in situations, and that makes you more stressed. The cycle is continued as you "give in" to your feelings of stress and exhaustion. There are important concerns that you must address and solve, to be sure, but most often the minor events, which are not important enough to consume your energy, cause stress to build in your life.

After evaluating what upsets you for one week, spend the next seven days determining how you will respond to situations before they occur instead of overreacting and adding unneeded stress.

12. Practice good time management.

The following checklist describes a few of the time-related problems parents often encounter. Put a check beside those that are a concern for you.

Time Management Survey

_____ My time is not my own.

_____ I am under chronic overload and always have more to do than time available.

_____ I have difficulty separating work and home.

_____ When I'm at home, I feel guilty that I am not working.

_____ When I'm at work, I feel guilty that I am not at home with my children.

_____ I lose concentration when I'm with my children because I'm always thinking about other things I have to do.

_____ I have difficulty delegating to my children, so I do it all myself.

_____ I do not know how to say "no" to church or community activities that put me in overload, leaving no time for my spouse and children.

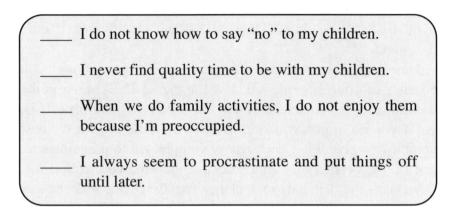

_____ I do not know how to say "no" to my children.

_____ I never find quality time to be with my children.

_____ When we do family activities, I do not enjoy them because I'm preoccupied.

_____ I always seem to procrastinate and put things off until later.

For many guilty parents, procrastination is probably the single biggest time management problem, but it can be stopped—if you act now. Many procrastinators are perfectionists just waiting for the "perfect" time to accomplish the task, yet others claim they perform better "under the gun." But procrastination only adds to daily stress.

Learn how to conquer procrastination and other time management problems by getting in the habit of planning your day. Set your priorities, schedule your commitments and household tasks for peak efficiency, and most important, establish small but attainable goals that will lessen your feelings of frustration and burnout. Chapter 7 offers specific suggestions related to setting priorities and goals.

Church: The Subtle Stressor

Other books fail to caution you against this subtle stress creator—or don't know to warn you at all. We have learned through years of experience in church ministry that church commitments can lead to overload. All three of us are committed to Christian service through the Bride of Christ, the church. However, we no longer allow our extra time to revolve solely around the church.

We know that Christ never intended for us to feel so tired and burned out "doing church" that we lose our sensitivity at "being the church."

Have you ever felt that the church was "punishing" you because of your giftedness and willingness? The church is the hardest place to remain faithful to the "one rule" (see page 117), yet if you do it, you will find that you are able to give the best you have to give. Find one activity you feel led to participate in, and be the best in that area God intended for you to become. Even with the demands of a clergy family, Debra still chooses one activity to participate in and gives it her best. Years ago, she would teach Sunday school, direct the children's choir, lead a young mothers' support group and more, only to realize that God did not intend for her to give her all at church and then be empty when her family came home.

Enjoy other one-time involvements, but guard against too many. For example, if you feel led to be a preschool Sunday school teacher, then limit your other volunteer efforts to providing transportation or food for a special event or calling church visitors for a limited time period. Then, be the best preschool Sunday school teacher you can be!

Gifted church members are often asked to serve on committees. However, if you are already teaching or volunteering in other ways, realize that committees will always be there, but your children will not. As they grow and your involvements change, you may want to consider additional service.

Often, we accept more commitments because we believe—or someone leads us to believe—that no one else will step forward to help. We feel guilty if we want to say "no," so we don't. But if God has led you to your ministry for the present, don't you think He will take care of another ministry that needs assistance? If we are honest, part of our feelings are self-inflicted guilt because down deep we want to take on one more thing and have the praise of fellow members. But it is just as important for your children to see you involved in ministry away from the church—visiting a sick neighbor or making a tape and card to send to Grandma—as it is for them to share in your church ministry.

Evaluate your church commitments. Are there some you need to reconsider and put aside for several years until your children are older? Saying "no" to overcommitment in church activities is often necessary—and it is possible. Celebrate God's love with your children at home. Enjoy using your home to reach out and demonstrate to your family how to care for others. Worship with your family without giving in to imposed guilt. And pray for God to show you the way He wants to use you.

Look for Hope

If you feel that you are over the line and are experiencing burnout, ask God to give you signs of hope. Look for small, brief moments of relief.

Ellen remembers the time she was a single mom in graduate school. She had to balance her time between going to class, holding a campus job, mothering, remaining active in church, staying involved in her children's school, and paying the bills. There was not much time for cultivating friendships or relaxing. She recalls:

> I would ask God to show me some sign of hope that I could make it. I desperately wanted a visible sign that He loved me. God answered my prayer in an unusual way. I started parking in a different place and walking a farther distance to class. The campus grounds were full of trees and squirrels. The scenery changed with the seasons. But it was a small bush that He used to give me hope. I passed the same bush every day all winter and then began to see tiny spots of green appear and grow each day. I made sure to check it

every time I passed for more new growth. Each new leaf seemed to restore a small amount of hope within me. When it was in full bloom, I felt such strength and knew beyond any doubt that God loved me and was in control of my life.

Hope is tenacious and eternal. Ask God to give some eternal signs to help you "hang in there." Understand that it takes time to heal from burnout. It takes time to trust people again.

Yes, we've been there. We've been physically, emotionally, mentally, and spiritually tired. But we have also found inner peace with the Great Physician. Remember, He sent a burning bush to Moses and a budding bush to Ellen. He will answer your prayer and give you hope.

When you begin to heal, we want you to make one more important commitment: Commit to *never* overcommit. As you continue to heal, remember the pain you experienced when you gave in to your guilt by doing more and more for everyone except yourself. Protect yourself and your family. Allow God to balance your life with fun, ministry, and hope.

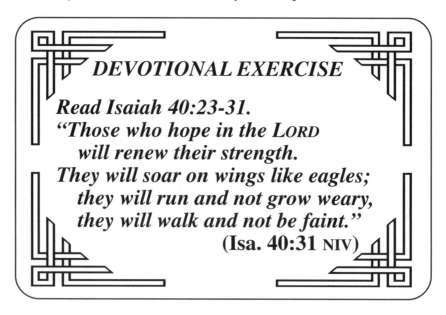

DEVOTIONAL EXERCISE

Read Isaiah 40:23-31.
"Those who hope in the LORD
will renew their strength.
They will soar on wings like eagles;
they will run and not grow weary,
they will walk and not be faint."
(Isa. 40:31 NIV)

It is our belief that overcommitted parents model burnout and stress for their children. What kind of heritage will you pass down to your children? It is hard to deal with the stress that inevitably attacks their lives when you have trouble dealing with your own. *Now* is the time to get it under control. With God's help, you can avoid parenting burnout!

GUILT-FREE CHALLENGES

1. Have you fought stress so long that you don't know how to live without it? What do you do for "recovery" or relaxation? If you do not know how to recover from a stressful day, chances are, your children won't know either. Relaxation is one of the fun things we model for our children. Are they learning it from you? Chart your stress for one week and record its causes. Then find small ways to give yourself temporary relief, such as playing your favorite CD or taking a walk—alone!

2. A major key to prevent burnout is to simplify your lifestyle. What would that mean for you and your family? Make a list of minor changes that would help to simplify your life; then make a list of major changes you might consider. Talk with your spouse or a trusted professional or friend about the possibilities. Start making the minor changes first, and very gradually work toward making the more difficult changes.

3. Observe your children. How often are they irritable because of schedule changes and too many commitments? Do they complain of being tired? Alleviate some of their activities by allowing them to be children. Continuous activity leads to mental atrophy. Encourage your children to use their ability to create and imagine—two important tasks of childhood. Then allow yourself the pleasure of daydreaming and imagining again! If you cannot literally "get away from it all" by taking a trip, you can at least imagine where you will go one day.

4. Whenever you begin to experience burnout, call a halt to your activities. Take time to thank God for what He has done for you. Has He helped you to hang on when life got tough? Has God provided a friend just when you didn't think you could go on? Has God wrapped His arms around you and held you in quietness as you cried? Make a list of what God has done for you. Add to it and read it daily. Remembering God's greatness and love will renew your strength.

5. What attributes do people have who maintain a sense of calm in their lives and relationships? Read the following attributes outlined in the book *Little House on the Freeway* and see if you need to make an attitude adjustment.

People who maintain a sense of calm . . .

* strive for simplicity

* laugh a lot

* are committed to obeying God's Word

* have thankful hearts

* try to bring the best out of the people they love the most

* dream big dreams

* let God do their worrying for them.[4]

Chapter 7

Set Priorities and Goals

*S*etting priorities and goals is one of the best ways to keep parenting pressures from overwhelming you and leading to burnout. When you recognize your abilities and limitations and have a clear understanding of the priorities in your life, you are then able to set goals and make commitments you can fulfill—without too much stress! Only then are you able to effectively reduce negative parenting guilt.

Review Your Priorities

The key to relieving parenting guilt can be described in one word: *balance*. Regaining a sense of personal equilibrium and internal stability is the secret to feeling confident as a person and as a parent. Reviewing your priorities, making choices, and budgeting your time each day according to those priorities are the first steps in achieving this balance in your life.

Setting priorities also helps to keep your life in perspective. In other words, knowing your priorities helps you to focus on the things that are most important and pay less attention to the others. For Christians, this means putting our relationship with Jesus Christ first, followed by personal relationships with our spouses and children. Remember what Paul told the Philippians: "What I once thought was valuable is worthless. . . . I have given up everything else and count it all as garbage. All I want is . . . to know that I belong . . . because of my faith in Christ" (Phil. 3:7-9 CEV).

Use the Commitment and Priority Worksheet on page 134 to help get your life into focus. Under the heading "My Commitments," list all of the activities, organizations, and commitments to which you devote yourself. Be sure to include tasks that you must do, such as work-related commitments, parenting, caregiving to aging parents, and housework. Also include activities that you do for your own pleasure and well-being, such as drawing, singing in the church choir, jogging, or gardening. When the list is complete, number the commitments from one to three according to this scale of importance:

#1 Those things you must do.
#2 Those things you should do.
#3 Those things that are of lesser importance.

Then write your commitments in three columns under the heading "My Priorities." A sample worksheet follows.

If you are a working parent, for example, staying employed is most likely a major commitment you must keep to provide for your family. In that case, you would put a #1 beside it and then list it under #1 Priority. Though you may not be able to eliminate this commitment from your priority list, you can regulate how many hours you work each week and avoid adding extra stress to your life by not overextending yourself with outside commitments.

Sample Commitment and Priority Worksheet

"My Commitments"

parenting	1	teach Sunday school	2
work	1	prayer and Bible study	1
housework	2	bowling with friends	3
marriage	1	sing in church choir	2
yard work	3	chair school carnival committee	3
daily exercise	3	homework with kids	2

"My Priorities"

#1 Priority	#2 Priority	#3 Priority
parenting	housework	yard work
work	homework with kids	daily exercise
marriage	teach Sunday school	bowling with friends
prayer and Bible study	sing in church choir	chair school carnival committee

Commitment and Priority Worksheet

"My Commitments"

"My Priorities"

#1 Priority   **#2 Priority**   **#3 Priority**

Many parents fall into the workaholic trap, never learning to delegate at the office or at home. Workaholics are commonly people who have set their career goals high; yet even homemakers can be workaholics as they work toward such goals as having the perfect child or a sparkling clean home or a successful committee. The truth is that workaholism can set you on the fast track to failure as your addiction to your work far surpasses what is most important in life—your faith and your family.

Completing the Commitment and Priority Worksheet will help you to determine if you are making your faith and your family top priorities or if you are allowing others to pull you away. If most of your commitments fall under #1 Priority, for example, you probably need to reevaluate the level of importance of each. Likewise, if the list of commitments under #2 Priority is long, you may need to reduce the number and variety of commitments you make. In either case, you are probably experiencing guilt caused by overextending yourself. It's time to think more carefully about how to modify your priorities.

As you seek to reprioritize your life in order to minimize unproductive guilt, read the following sample guilt audit and then complete your own on page 137.

Sample Guilt Audit

1. What guilt feelings are nagging at me?

   * I never have enough time for the kids.

   * The house never seems clean enough.

   * My child's grades are not good enough.

   * There is never enough money to buy the things we need (or want).

2. How can I avoid these guilt feelings?

* limit amount of overtime worked

* keep from overcommitting myself

* stop dwelling on personal imperfections

* allow kids to be "good enough"

3. What strategies can help me to make these changes?

* reorder my priorities, putting faith and family first

* set a watch alarm to remind me when it's time to leave the office

* post a calendar on the refrigerator to remind me of my commitments and help me to keep from over-committing

* learn to laugh more and enjoy my children more

* spend more time with my spouse

* focus on my positive qualities by listing them and taping them to my bathroom mirror

Personal Guilt Audit

1. What guilt feelings are nagging at me?

2. How can I avoid these guilt feelings?

3. What strategies can help me to make these changes?

Now reconsider your list of commitments and priorities on page 134. What changes do you need to make? How do the strategies you included in your guilt audit support these changes?

The Importance of Goal Setting

After completing these exercises, Kimberly realized that her commitments required more time than she had to give, leaving her feeling guilty and stressed out. Yet when she reviewed her list of commitments and priorities, she stopped midstream. "There is not one thing I would like to remove from my list," she said honestly. "I love everything I do. The problem is that there is not enough time or energy to do it all."

Making adjustments in our commitments is not always easy, even when we truly want to keep our priorities "in order." Most of us enjoy staying busy and having many commitments. You have probably heard the saying, "If you want something done, ask a busy person." For whatever reason, many of us— especially women—thrive on juggling all the responsibilities of home and family. One study found that although nine out of ten women reported having time pressures in their lives, more than 75 percent also said that they enjoy all aspects of "their current full, busy lives."[1]

Yet when our commitments exceed the number of hours in the day, there is a problem. As Kimberly discovered, this problem leads to excessive stress and, ultimately, to burnout. And when a parent is burned out, he or she is not helpful to anyone, including self.

Several years ago, Debra tells of committing to write three books at one time while editing a bimonthly newspaper, caring for her family, and volunteering at church. She recalls:

When my agent contracted me to write the books, it was very exciting. I loved researching and writing on each subject; however, as deadlines began to creep up, I felt intense pressure. With some rearranging of responsibilities and schedules, I got through this tense period with the support of Bob and the kids. I've now learned to set goals in advance and prioritize my time so that I don't feel high stress and excess guilt.

Debra learned the hard way that goal setting is necessary if we are to keep our priorities in focus and reduce parenting guilt, especially when too many commitments are causing pressure.

All three of us have experienced that setting goals can help you turn your dreams into reality—if you pursue your goals without diversions. Once you have reviewed your priorities, setting goals can help you to support those priorities by choosing specifically "where you want to go." By knowing precisely what you want to achieve ahead of time, you know what you have to concentrate on and improve. You also can see what distractions you face. Goal setting gives you long-term vision and short-term motivation, focuses your acquisition of knowledge, and helps you to organize your resources.

Set Personal and Family Goals

Deciding what goals are important to your life and the life of your family is a very powerful technique that can yield strong returns in all areas of your life. Without specific goals, you and your family have no guidelines by which to measure your growth—qualitative or quantitative. You also are much more likely to live with nagging guilt if you don't have a general plan of where you and your family are headed in life.

Although there is no quick fix for alleviating parenting guilt, Ellen has learned that setting personal and family goals is extremely helpful. In her work and extra activities, Ellen refuses to jeopardize family time. She works hard not to bring work home and says "no" if church meetings begin to claim more time than her family. She shares:

My kids are teenagers. Some days I cannot remember how they got that old and that tall. It is like we just woke up one morning, and they were grown. Stuart and Emily are gifted, opinionated young people discovering who God wants them to be and making a difference in the world. I just can't afford to miss this life stage. We work too hard as parents getting them to a semi-independent stage to miss out on this. I enjoy the spontaneous times of family fun the most. If I weren't around, I would miss a family game of Trivial Pursuit or Movie Mania. And I can't miss a game, because one day I might actually win!

Robert and Debra have worked toward achieving two main goals as they have raised their three children. One has been encouraging a personal relationship with God through Jesus Christ. The other has been providing them with an excellent education. Aside from these two goals, everything else has weighed low on their list of parenting priorities through the years, including expensive vacations and designer clothing.

Whatever goals you set for yourself and your family, having godly goals that support godly priorities is fundamental. The book of Proverbs reminds us of this: "In everything you do, put God first, and he will direct you and crown your efforts with success" (3:6 TLB). This is especially important when the day's activities and circumstances add to your guilt feelings. By keeping your focus on your Maker and His priorities for your life, you can remain hopeful that all things will work toward His glory.

Start with a Family Meeting

Regular family meetings are a good way to set and review personal and family goals. They also are an excellent tool for keeping communication open and addressing problems of family

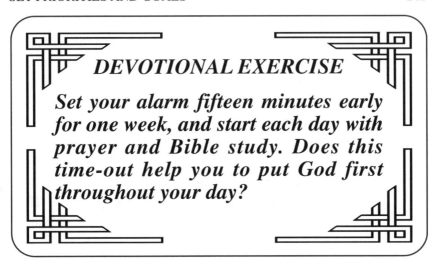

DEVOTIONAL EXERCISE

Set your alarm fifteen minutes early for one week, and start each day with prayer and Bible study. Does this time-out help you to put God first throughout your day?

members. You may choose to meet weekly, biweekly, or monthly with your family; in any case, the following guidelines will be helpful:

1. Talk with your family members about their expectations. Work together to set short-term, or immediate, family goals as well as long-term family goals, which might take months or even years to achieve. A short-term goal might be to budget money to buy a new computer program in two weeks or to give more attention to home responsibilities if one person is not doing her or his share. Delegating household responsibilities so that one person is not feeling the brunt of chores each day is a viable goal for busy families. A long-term goal might be to save enough money to go on vacation during the summer. Another long-term goal for a two-parent family might be paring down to live on one income so that one parent can stay home with the children.

In addition to focusing on short- and long-term family goals, consider personal goals. (If your children are old enough, you might have them set personal goals, too.) What would you like to achieve personally? Where are you headed with your career? With your spiritual life? Perhaps you need to begin an exercise program, which would be both a short- and a long-term goal.

When you set goals, whether they are personal or family goals, make sure that you consider the time involved to attain each goal. Don't confuse daily goals, short-term goals, and long-term goals. When you set attainable goals, you ensure that the goals are within your reach. Perfectionists usually try to outdo the world by reaching for goals that are far too difficult. Then when faced with failure, they feel personal humiliation, adding to their stress and guilt.

2. Ask, What would it take to make these goals happen? The Bible teaches that faith without works is dead. This same concept is true of personal and family goals. Meeting your goals involves putting action behind them.

As you talk with your family, discuss ways to make your goals a reality. If tightening the budget is a goal, talk about practical ways to do this, using suggestions from chapter 9. If becoming more physically active is a goal, designate family exercise time when you ride bikes or jog together. If your personal goal is to make time daily to work on a special hobby, talk with family members about how you are going to do this and ask for their help.

If at any time you realize that a time crunch is adding to your already burdened day, then you can work toward evaluating your goals and establishing new ones—within reasonable parameters that you can achieve.

3. Review these goals regularly at your family meeting. Even if your children are young, it is important to meet regularly as a family. We know how difficult this can be, for every family member has her or his own activities or responsibilities, but you must make your family meeting a priority in your home. Regular reviews will allow you to keep goals in the forefront, so that they are more likely to happen. For example, if you decide to save money for a family vacation but do not discuss this goal for months, chances are it will never happen. Goals need to be reviewed, celebrated, and put into action—with everyone being involved.

4. As you meet your goals, set new ones. Evaluate the success of each goal, and determine where you should go from here. New goals do not have to be extravagant or "bigger and better" than the previous goals; rather, they should focus on bringing your life and your family's life into balance.

Making It Happen

Reviewing your priorities and setting goals are necessary steps to balancing your life as you strive to be a "good enough" parent. Yet sometimes you may slip back into old habits and routines. Here are a few tips to help you reach your goals and uphold your priorities.

Stick to Your Daily "To Do" List

Scheduling your day for peak efficiency is the best way to "get in control" of how you spend your time. Are you an early bird or a night owl? Whenever possible, schedule tasks according to your energy cycle and circadian or internal rhythms (see page 98).

Almost everyone engages in problematic behaviors at least some of the time, including:

* rushing

* staying busy

* responding to every need that presents itself

* letting our lives get out of balance

* procrastinating

* feeling our time is not our own

* trying to earn the love of others, even God

There is no reason to judge ourselves harshly for these human tendencies. However, we can view these behaviors as golden opportunities to gain an understanding of what we might change in order to experience the abundant life that is God's will for us.[2]

To gain control of your time each day, write a "to do" list of all the tasks that face you that day, including activities that you choose to do for self-improvement or personal enjoyment. Budget ample time for each task by calculating how long it will take you to complete it. When her children were young, Debra always added an extra fifteen to thirty minutes to each project, allowing herself to work at a moderate speed instead of in high gear. The extra time gave her some leeway, especially on days when interruptions such as a crying baby or a stubborn child held her back from optimum performance.

If you have more tasks scheduled than time available, rewrite your "to do" list and prioritize the projects that must be done that day, putting the less important projects or activities at the bottom of the list. Projects that are not immediate can always wait until another day, or you can delegate them to family members. Sharing the load is crucial as you learn to balance your day, doing what you can without overextending yourself.

Some busy parents prefer to make their "to do" lists each morning, while others are like Robert, who finds that doing this the night before when the family is in bed relieves his mind and enables him to sleep more soundly.

A word of warning: Some parents get so caught up in the routine of their day that they cannot be flexible. As wizened parents, we know that being flexible is integral to riding the storms of life. If you have planned your day and this plan is interrupted unexpectedly, *revamp your plan.*

Think Before Making New Commitments

As you work on setting priorities and goals in your family, each family member should make a commitment to assign reasonable limits to her or his time. Set an example by reviewing the list of commitments you made on page 134 and, as much as possible, eliminating those that are not absolutely necessary. You may have to give up a special interest if it conflicts with responsibilities such as helping with homework or being with your spouse. Of course, you may have to see through some short-term commitments, but you can think twice before making any new commitments. For example, you can think twice before volunteering for another night committee, especially if you are at work all day and family awaits you at night.

Guilt-free parenting is all about getting your priorities in order so that everyone wins—including you. Yes, it may take some sacrifice now and then, but in the long run, you will feel better and function better knowing that the important needs—the things that really matter in life—are being met.

As you accept what you cannot change in your life and focus on the strengths you identified on page 54, remember that you don't have to be all things to all people. You can be "good enough" as a parent and still affirm and love your children—with no regrets.

Robert remembers trying to fulfill the role of Super Dad while coaching three Little League teams, never taking time for himself:

I wanted the kids to feel that I supported their commitment to sports, so I volunteered to be the coach—of each child's team. Every afternoon at 3:30 I would leave the church, pick up the kids from school, and go to the Little League field to coach T-ball, girls' softball, or baseball practice. I spent my nights and weekends coaching the games, while also serving as senior pastor of a large church. Now that I look back, I wonder how I could have ever done so much. It seemed appropriate at the time, but now I know that I didn't have to do it all. I should have taken it slower, enjoyed life more, and appreciated my children without leading an overly committed, fast-paced life.

As we have said previously, lowering your expectations as a parent does *not* mean throwing in the towel. Rather, it means realizing that you are one person with limited energy. You can do some things, but you cannot do it all. Remember, Jethro advised Moses to share the workload to protect Moses and his people from stress and weariness. Sometimes we must share or even eliminate some of our workload or stress in order to get rid of feelings of entrapment.

Jesus reminds us to count the cost before taking on anything new (Luke 14:28-33). As we read in Matthew 5:37, we must let our *yes* be *yes* and our *no* be *no*.

Learn to Say "No"

If there is one thing that most guilty parents have in common, it is a failure to say "no." As we have shown, failing to set limits or say "no" to too many demands will put you in overload and add to your already rising stress level as a parent. Remember your Comfort Zone and Uncomfortable Zone? We believe that it is much easier to make decisions that involve a physical and mental commitment *in advance* by identifying your talents and limitations. It is much easier to say "no" to a persuasive friend when you have thought about the situation beforehand.

Keep on hand copies of your Comfort Zone and Uncomfortable Zone, your Commitment and Priority Worksheet, and your personal and family goals. When someone asks you to do something, whether serving on a committee or teaching a class, review your lists and weigh the pros and cons, including family members in the discussion. Ask yourself, Would another commitment keep me from doing the things in my Comfort Zone—keep me from focusing on my God-given talents? Would it divert me from the priorities that are foremost on my list, such as my faith development and nurturing my family? Would it fit easily into my plan of short- and long-term goals? If not, politely refuse. The desire to help others is commendable, but if being all things to all people is making you feel resentful, tired, or even depressed, it is time to take a firm stand. Say "no" and mean it.

Remember, saying "no" is the polar opposite of saying "yes," and it takes practice. We know that being honest with people when saying "no" is often difficult, especially for enthusiastic Christians. If you are completely honest, people will accuse you of being blunt and inconsiderate. "Don't you care about our class (or group or cause)?" they ask. On the other hand, if you hide your feelings and commit yourself to anyone who asks for your involvement, you will resent the activity, and this resentment will show. Your participation will begin to reflect a phony and insincere attitude. The key to saying "no" lies in being honest but tactful. As we have said, you will feel stronger physically and emotionally if you make only commitments that you can keep without undue stress.

Increase Communication Skills

Recognizing that you and every member of your family have personal limitations, try to keep communication within the family open. The purpose is to better understand one another's expectations, needs, feelings, and interests.

Regularly set aside time to talk with your spouse and each child—alone. You can discuss problems and specific needs. If spending time alone is difficult, use letter writing or the telephone to stay in touch with each person's needs. Even calling your spouse at work for a fifteen-second greeting is time well spent!

You may find it productive to ask each family member to do the exercise on page 88 to discover his or her own Comfort Zone and Uncomfortable Zone. Compare lists at your next family meeting, and delegate responsibilities so that family members are doing more things in their Comfort Zones than responsibilities they don't enjoy.

Make Time to Have Fun

As your children see you live the Christian life throughout the week, show them that it is a life of joy, promise, and celebration. The psalmist says, "O taste and see that the LORD is good! / Happy is the man who takes refuge in him!" (Ps. 34:8 RSV). When Alicia read that verse at a parent support group, she was honestly surprised that parents were "allowed" to celebrate and be happy. Unfortunately, laughing and celebrating amidst the clutter of daily living are difficult for most of us. At the end of the day, when all is said and done, can you say that you have enjoyed your life? When you climb into bed at night, can you say that you have laughed that day?

As we live day by day with parenting guilt, along with the pressures of making ends meet, some of us lose that carefree spirit. We recommend letting the "parent guard" down once in a while. Although your home is structured for discipline, it is also a place for celebration and fellowship. In our own homes, laughter is frequent, enabling our family members to feel good about being alive.

Remember the fun times you used to have as a child? Perhaps it was bowling on Saturday morning or fishing late at night or having a picnic on the beach and watching the sunset. Making time to have fun in your family enhances the parent-child relationship. Your fun times might be free or inexpensive and spur of the moment—such as having an early breakfast at a nearby restaurant before school or watching the late movie together on Saturday night. No matter how you "play" these light moments, they are vital in continuing the joy and spontaneity that you experienced as a child—joy that you want to pass on to your children!

Know When to Say It Is "Good Enough"

Setting priorities and goals relieves some of the nagging guilt of parenting as you learn to say, "Yes, this is good enough." As we have said previously, "good enough" means deciding what is most important to your family and what is less important. Is it worth having gourmet meals if you are exhausted at the end of the day? Are shining kitchen countertops important if your children are afraid to come into "Mom's clean kitchen"? Is it worth working full-time, putting children in day care and having high anxiety, if one parent makes a "good enough" income and the other could stay home? Ask yourself, What will my children remember? Will they remember how sparkling clean your kitchen floor was or how much they enjoyed the long walk after school? Will they remember that you fixed gourmet meals each night or that you really listened when they wanted to talk?

Once you have determined what is most important in the life of your family, focus on these priorities. Because your family is unique, your priorities will be, too. What is important to you may have lesser importance to someone else. But with your focus on Jesus Christ as the number one priority for a Christ-centered home, you can sort through your many commitments and do the very things that have meaning.

Let God Lead the Way

Do you know people whose lives are totally in place? They never seem to be rushed. They enjoy their family time together.

They don't worry about the future, and they attribute even their smallest successes to God. These special people live in God and for God. They have learned the secret to living guilt-free—the realization that when one reserves time to celebrate God's goodness, the rest of life falls into place.

A story is told of a mental hospital where the doctors developed an unusual test to determine when their patients were ready to go back into society. They would bring the patient being considered for release into a room with a sink. When the patient entered the room, the faucet over the sink was already turned on. The sink was overflowing, and water was pouring onto the floor. The patient was handed a mop and asked to clean up the mess. If the patient had enough sense to turn off the faucet before starting to mop up the water, the doctors concluded that he was ready to go back into society. However, if he started mopping while the water was still running, more treatment was needed.

Parents must stop mopping long enough to look up and see if the faucet is still running. How does that relate to guilty parents? We need to go to the root of our hurried, guilty lives and find out what is holding us back from experiencing the freedom that comes with God's grace. We have crowded God out of our lives. Without God, life is simply a whirlwind of meaningless activity. To regain control at home and relieve ourselves of negative guilt, we must center our lives in God and His purpose. Does a loving, Christian atmosphere permeate your home? A family that is secured in God's love through Jesus Christ will be eternal: "A threefold cord is not quickly broken" (Eccles. 4:12 RSV).

Being a Christian parent is not an easy task, especially in today's world. However, as you make time to set goals for yourself and your family, with God leading the way, you can begin to experience this ultimate sense of hope and purpose.

GUILT-FREE CHALLENGES

1. On busy days, do you experience symptoms of stress or burnout? Make it a priority to schedule your day so that "downtime" is included, making sure that the activities and commitments you plan do not exceed the number of hours in the day.

2. As you prepare your daily "to do" lists, be sure to schedule for your "peak time" the activities that require you to be alert. For example, if you are an early bird, do the things that require concentration in the morning. If you are a night owl, you will want to save the activities for afternoon or evening.

3. To effectively manage your time, recognize how you spend the hours of each day. Draw a circle and divide it into pielike sections. Let this circle represent your life of the past month. Fill in the percentage of time you spent doing the following:

*criticizing self   *affirming self
*affirming those around you   *helping others
*worrying   *reading scriptures
*praying for self and others

What changes are needed?

4. How difficult is it to say "no" to those who want more of your time than you are willing to give? Write down several ways you can say "no" to persistent friends or solicitors, and

tape this to the wall by your telephone. Use these statements when you are overcommitted.

5. To grow as a "guilt-free" parent takes time, but there has to be a starting point. Let today be your official "starting point" as you chart your parenting journey. Draw a horizontal line and number it from 1 to 10, with 1 representing "guilty parent" and 10 representing "guilt-free parent." Circle and label the numbers that represent your feelings and behaviors one year ago, six months ago, one month ago, last week, and today. Have you been moving forward, standing still, or going backward in your parenting journey? Where would you like to be six months from now? A year from now? Set some specific, realistic goals to help you get there.

Chapter 8

Allow Your Child to Be All God Intends

*A*s we work toward becoming guilt-free parents, the Scriptures give us great strength. In Proverbs 22:6, we find instruction and assurance: "Train up a child in the way he should go, / and when he is old he will not depart from it" (RSV). Most of us agree that training is vital in creating a positive, self-confident child, but the question is, Did God really create all His children to "go" the same way?

Some Bible scholars have suggested that in the original Hebrew, the intent of this passage is "Train up a child according to his or her bent." The root word has to do with the bent of a tree. For instance, a willow tree that leans over a pond toward the southern sun is bent in a certain way. If we try to force it to bend in another way, we will break it.[1]

Accepting each child in the family according to God's plan is a crucial aspect of guilt-free parenting. We do this by nurturing each child in a manner that "follows his or her bent," realizing that child's special gifts and talents without forcing our personal desires upon him or her.

Instead of always allowing our children to follow their "bent," however, we all are guilty of having inappropriate expectations of our children. In fact, sometimes we try to live vicariously through our children. Then when they choose to follow a different path, we are faced with great disappointment. In these cases, we work diligently to "fix" our children when we are the ones who need to be fixed.

Is it conceivable that we can "fix" parenting guilt when our children do not follow our dream but lean toward their special "bent" in life? We know it is. *And you can do it* by beginning to really understand your child, focus on your child's strengths, and have realistic expectations of the child rather than comparing him or her to anyone else.

Ellen tells about a memorable experience when her daughter was young:

I picked up Emily from her Wednesday night preschool class at church. That night her class focused on 1 Thessalonians 4:11: "Work with your hands" (NIV). As Emily bounded out of the classroom, she proudly presented me with her handprints painted on a piece of construction paper with the Bible verse from 1 Thessalonians printed at the bottom.

On the way home, we had an unusually mature discussion for a mom and a three-year-old. Emily was eager to expound on her hopes and dreams for using her hands. As if she had pondered the question for years, she asked me if I knew what she wanted to be when she "got big."

"I want to be a doctor," Emily said with confidence.

Thinking that was quite a bold dream for a little girl, I listened closely as she continued to share her dreams.

"But when I get even bigger, I want to be a ballerina."

This dream sounded more typical of a preschooler, but Emily was not through: "But, Mommy, do you know what I want to be when I get really, really big? I want to be a missionary [pronounced mis-son-ary]."

Trying to control her giggles as she imagined this tiny dancing missionary with a stethoscope dangling around her neck, Ellen gave her blessings to the three possibilities because she was having so much fun dreaming with her child.

We all can relate to little Emily. We spend our whole lives dreaming about what we want to be when we are older. Children often change their minds about what they want to be as their interests and abilities change; so do adults. Allowing your child to become all God intends is not about seeking what your child will become when he or she is an adult. It is about the developmental process you allow your child to go through to help him or her get there.

It may surprise you that the big decision about "becoming" belongs not to your child but to you. Your biggest choice is whether you will allow your child to become what God intends for him or her to be, rather than what you want him or her to be. Unless you purposely choose the former, some threatening syndromes can consciously or subconsciously influence your child's ability to become all God intends:

Syndrome #1
I want my child to be better than I was.

Syndrome #2
I want my child to be the best.

Syndrome #3
I want my child to be happy.

Let's consider each of these syndromes briefly before exploring how to overcome them.

Syndrome #1: I Want My Child to Be Better Than I Was

It is not unusual for parents to want their children to have it better than they had it. Many parents who grew up during the depression have been criticized for pushing their children to succeed. Lynn Marie's family is a good example.

Lynn Marie, a thirty-nine-year-old mother of three, never finished college because her parents kept pushing her to get a degree. Neither one of her parents was able to finish college. Her mother's family could not afford it; her dad never had the opportunity to complete his degree after the war ended. Lynn Marie remembers:

> Education was the main goal my parents had for us. Nothing was as important as our grades. Anytime any of us received a grade lower than a B, we were punished. I missed my senior prom because I made a C in algebra and was grounded. School was not difficult for me because I was a strong student, but my brothers were not. They were constantly being pushed and punished and made to feel unworthy of all my parents provided for them.

Lynn Marie completed her freshman and sophomore years of college, then dropped out suddenly and got married. She says she married mainly to escape her parents' pressure. She became pregnant right after her first anniversary, and money has been tight ever since. Both of her brothers joined the army and never attempted to pursue higher education.

We have seen so many parents who feel inferior to their peers—financially, socially, or educationally—and use their children in an effort to relieve some of these feelings of inferiority. Perhaps the parents want their children to have an opportunity they never had. Or perhaps they had a chance to become something more and wasted it. In either case, to compensate for their "loss," these parents constantly drive their children to succeed. Failure is not tolerated; risk is a waste of time. These parents want to raise successful children to absolve their own guilt that continually reminds them that, in their eyes, they are not "a success."

Syndrome #2: I Want My Child to Be the Best

Tim and Kristen are parents who are obsessed with being the best. Before age thirty, Tim rose the corporate ladder to an upper management position. Not long after the promotion, he and his family moved from a comfortable home in a quiet middle-income neighborhood to a newly built subdivision where the houses range from expensive to extravagant. The large boost in their house note made it necessary for his wife, Kristen, to make the move from part-time to full-time employment.

Tim and Kristen have three "model children." Their son is the captain of the football team. Their third-grade daughter has already won several piano honors, and their five-year-old daughter excels in gymnastics and dance. She even performed a solo routine at her dance studio's recital in the city convention center. Each child is told to be the best in his or her selected interest. But selected by whom?

On his own high school football team, Tim was always the team manager instead of a player. Even before having children, he was determined that his firstborn son would be a star football player in high school, get recruited for a college football scholarship, and go on to the National Football League (NFL). Tim is doing all he can to encourage his son to pursue that dream. Likewise, Kristen's parents wanted her to have a career in dance or music, but she chose to be a nurse instead. Now she encourages her daughters to focus their talents in the arts.

The family used to have more time for family trips and projects, but life is now extremely fast-paced with each child having a different practice schedule. Tim and Kristen, however, count that as a small sacrifice for obtaining their goals. They are fueled by the blessings and praises given by extended family, colleagues, and even church leaders.

Even though their family may appear to "have it all," Tim and Kristen's yearning for their family to *be* the best is much different from wanting or expecting their family to *do* their best. Despite popular belief, children *can* be encouraged to do their best even in competitive situations. But to Tim and Kristen, life is a constant race in which the best family wins the gold. Their drive to eliminate their own guilt about "never measuring up" will eventually drive their children away from them because the children cannot bear the performance pressure their parents have forced them to live with. Although the children might rebel against the way they were raised, because it is the only pattern they know, the percentage is high that they, too, will raise "guilty" kids.

Syndrome #3: I Want My Child to Be Happy

Linda had a "Beaver Cleaver" upbringing. Her family lived in the typical suburban two-story home with the white picket fence. Her mother drove the wood-paneled station wagon. Weekends were spent visiting family and friends, and the family never missed a Sunday at church. No one close to Linda died when she was growing up, and if her family ever had any problems, she never heard about them. In fact, people used to compliment them on how perfect they were. Linda learned later in life that her dad could sometimes be very domineering toward her mom, so Linda's mom tried to keep everything running smoothly while smiling outwardly.

Today Linda's idea of parenting is going the second or even third mile to make sure everyone is happy. Her family does not discuss unpleasant matters, watch any kind of negative programming, or associate with anyone who has known problems. Linda believes that she will never be as good a mother as her own mother, so she continues to lavish her children with gifts, special activities, and her time. She has been room mother for the last four years and will serve next year as PTA president. She tries to make cookies at least twice a week in between driving the car pool daily and taking her children to their latest activity. After several weeks, when the kids get bored with one activity, Linda quickly pulls another rabbit from her hat to excite them.

Linda's children are actually good kids, but they seem to complain and whine a lot at church and school. Their teachers say it's because their mother is a martyr, and teachers can't afford to give constant attention to one child when there are twenty others in the classroom. They hesitate to talk to Linda about the kids because they are grateful that she so willingly gives of her time to the school.

While Linda is not a bad mother, she is allowing guilt to distort her parenting priorities. Her parental role—and ours—is to raise emotionally healthy children who can function independently and also contribute to their own families and communities.

By trying to prevent her children from experiencing the difficulties and setbacks that are part of life, Linda is falling short of her responsibilities as a parent. We believe that "small whiners grow up to be tall complainers" because they have developed no "struggle muscle." They constantly search for friends and a spouse who will take care of them just like Mom (or, perhaps, Dad) did. These frustrated people never struggled with who they were or who they would become because that was hard work, and after all, Mom did all the work.

We have observed that guilty parents are often hand-wringing parents who overreact to situations that their children need to solve for themselves. Yet raising children who are able to function in the world using their talents and abilities means backing off and letting our children become responsible for their own actions—and consequences. It means breaking the "helicopter parent" pattern, which keeps us hovering over our young, waiting to rescue them from failure or frustration. Obviously, children need to experience frustration, setbacks, and even disappointments in order to become responsible adults. That's how they learn to cope, regroup, and try again when life gets tough. And as you may have experienced, life will get tough!

Curing the Dysfunctional Parenting Syndrome

Is it wrong to want your child to have a better life than you had? Is it really a problem to seek the best for your child and treasure her or his successes? And what could possibly be wrong with wanting your child to be happy? After all, we like being happy!

If kept in perspective, none of these is a wrong desire for you to have for your children. But if one of these scenarios becomes a top priority, you may have a guilt-inflicted infection we like to call Dysfunctional Parenting Syndrome (D.P.S.). You can count on D.P.S. to cause either a present-day or a future catastrophe. The actual catastrophe will not be the problem; rather, the problem will be your inability to deal with the catastrophe, along with the grave impact that will have on your children and your children's children. In many cases, "surgery" is highly recommended (in other words, the removal of the cause of D.P.S.). Long-term emotional and spiritual treatment is the only cure. In other words, to get rid of D.P.S., you must get rid of the guilt!

To alleviate inappropriate parenting guilt, George Barna encourages us to watch some reruns of programs that were popular in the late 1950s and 1960s. Barna suggests that while watching these shows, notice what the traditional family looked like and what they talked about. Watch how the parents interacted with each other and their children. Barna declares that "as sanitized as they were, those old shows delivered a subtle yet powerful message" about the family as an essential part of the American dream.[2]

The message of what it means to be a family is often confused or muffled today. The predictability that formerly defined the family seems to be lost forever. Though we can purposefully plan to bring *consistency* back to our family life, we cannot return to the days of Ozzie and Harriet or Rob and Laura. Our parenting guilt will not bring back the Cleavers' world.

Building a family atmosphere around guilt makes it extremely difficult for children to grow into healthy, whole adults. Anger, shame, repression, or depression clouds their young, vulnerable lives as they are directed by our sense of failure. Yet Jesus' words give us hope: "I have come that they may have life, and have it to the full" (John 10:10 NIV). The good news is that parenting is *not* about success or failure. Rather, it is about an abundant relationship with the One who can relieve our guilt and give us radiant new life.

To establish this relationship, our most important parenting task is to teach our children about God—a God of "beginning again." Consider how you are presently helping your children to experience God's best for their lives. You'll find specific ideas in the next section. You don't want you to miss this great opportunity and blessing to become all God intended you to be as a parent!

Before reading more about how to build up your children, what about you? Are you following your "bent"? Consider the following as you do a personal evaluation:

* As a child, what did you dream of becoming when you were grown?

* How many times did your dream change?

* Are you happy with your life at this time?

* If not, what changes need to be made to make you happy?

To help you answer the last question, we suggest you conduct your own research using the following guidelines and work-sheet:

* Make an appointment with a minister, psychologist, or career counselor.

* Take a personality test to find out what your strengths are.

* Ask trusted friends what they see as your strengths. If you are brave enough, ask about your weaknesses, too.

* Ask relatives what you enjoyed during childhood.

* Make a list below of what you like and dislike about your life, such as your job or daily routine.

* Determine what you can change and create a plan to accomplish this.

My Life Worksheet

Likes:	Dislikes:	Changes to make:
1.		
2.		
3.		
4.		
5.		
6.		
7.		
8.		
9.		
10.		

As *you* strive to become all God intended you to be, you become a better parent—free from guilt and D.P.S., free to help your children become all God intends.

From Hindrances to Help

For many of us, the issue is not what we are doing *wrong* to hinder our children but what we should be doing *right* to help them. Most of us really want to be sure we are helping our children become all God intends. So, how can we build up our children?

Step #1: Knowing

First, you cannot help your child to be all God intends if you don't personally *know God*. Nothing is more life-changing than knowing the One who formed you. No corporation, bank, school, neighbor, church, or child is more important than your relationship with God through Jesus Christ.

We know all the excuses for not nurturing a growing relationship with God because we have used them all, too. So let's skip the "I would if . . . " list and offer some suggestions for busy parents like you and like us.

* Give up one thirty-minute TV show (or activity) a day to find quiet time for God.

* Get up before the rest of the family does and spend the time in study and prayer.

* Read your Bible before you turn off the light at night.

* Keep a devotional book in your magazine stack. Before you read about a physical makeover, commit to reading one devotional for a quick spiritual makeover.

* Tape a "scripture for the week" on your car visor, your bathroom mirror, or your refrigerator. Try to memorize it before the week is over, and practice it in your daily life.

* Invite a friend to be your prayer partner. Call each other twice a week to share needs, insights, and updates and to pray together. Hold each other accountable for spending time with God.

* Agree with your spouse to read the same book or passage of scripture one week or month. At the end of the week, share what you have learned.

* Tell your children what you are learning from God and how you feel when you spend time with Him. They will be excited to hear about your relationship with the God who loves them.

* Start a support group for parents at your church. Help each other become all God intends.

If we're not careful, we can become immobilized by our guilt and never attempt to conquer our hectic schedules. Many of us are tempted to believe that we can make it without God and that we have failed God so much that we can never change. Yet God's message of grace assures us this is not true. God continues to desire a closer relationship with those He created and loves.

At Ellen's house there are two adults, two teenagers, and a baby. The baby is a four-year-old bichon frise named Jarvis. (For those who are not familiar with the bichon frise, it is a dog that looks much like a marshmallow!) At first glance, you wouldn't know how great Jarvis is because he is such a wimp. If you look at him with a glaring stare, he hides his tail between his legs. However, according to Ellen, Jarvis is more attached to her than any pet she has ever had. She explains:

I probably know Jarvis so well because we have an early morning routine seven days a week that helps to start our day.

We get up together at 4:50 A.M. (5:45 A.M. on weekends). He follows me to the bathroom, the kitchen, and the family room until he knows I am finally at the "getting dressed" stage; then he returns to Emily's bed for a little extra snoozing. I can honestly predict everything he is going to do in the mornings.

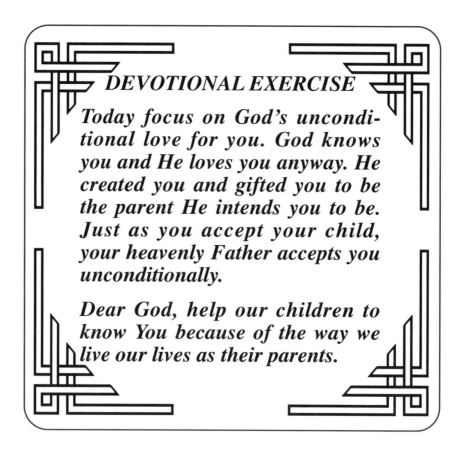

DEVOTIONAL EXERCISE

Today focus on God's unconditional love for you. God knows you and He loves you anyway. He created you and gifted you to be the parent He intends you to be. Just as you accept your child, your heavenly Father accepts you unconditionally.

Dear God, help our children to know You because of the way we live our lives as their parents.

Ellen and Jarvis are so attached to each other because they spend regular time together. Likewise, when we make the decision to spend regular time with God, we begin to have a deeper relationship with Him. The same holds true for our relationships with our children.

At every stage of their development, we must purposefully set aside time to listen and "be" with our children. It is amazing what we can learn from riding in the car with our children or with a car pool of our children's friends. Watching and listening to how our children interact with other children teach us a great deal. As we hear about things of interest to them, we learn more about their temperaments, their likes and dislikes, and their gifts. We also understand more about each child's "bent." Take a minute right now to think about what each child likes to do. Can you answer the following?

What holds my child's attention the longest?

What activities seem to bring my child the most pleasure?

What activities seem to come easier to my child?

What lessons has my child asked about for longer than six months?

What areas has my child's teacher said that he or she excels in?

The more we know about our children, the better we can respond to them in the most appropriate ways, motivating them to be the best they can be.

Step #2: Going

When you spend time getting to know God better, He will change *what you do and where you go.* He will lead you to people and situations that allow you to experience His best. It is assuring to remember that nothing is wasted in the life of a Christian. God uses each experience to teach you more about Him and more about yourself. However, you cannot learn these things by sitting in your recliner and praying twenty-four hours a day.

The same is true for your children. Another way to help each child be all God intended is to expose him or her to a variety of experiences and people. As your child tries new challenges, he or she will discover more about personal likes and dislikes and strengths and weaknesses.

Ellen remembers when a friend at church literally dragged her son, Stuart, to tryouts for their annual Broadway dinner play. Stuart had never been in a theatrical production and really didn't want to pursue it. However, he not only did well at the tryouts, but he also landed the lead male role in *Hello, Dolly!* Ellen recalls:

> We wondered who the kid was on the stage. Suddenly, our studious son was singing, dancing, and putting his arms around a girl. His success gave him the confidence to try out the next year. Last year, Stuart played the part of Professor Henry Higgins in *My Fair Lady.* But without moving out of his Comfort Zone, he would have never realized his talents.

God can use all types of experiences to help your child discover his or her full potential. Here are some experiences that might encourage growth in your child. Of course, your child has his or her own "bent," and you will know best how to modify activities or choose others that will be more effective with your child. Remember, involving your child in too many activities at one time can be detrimental to both of you!

1. Church programs that focus on biblical education, missions, and music can boost children's faith experience. A biblical education gives children a firm, spiritual foundation. Mission programs not only teach children about real families who devote themselves to serving God, but they also allow them to experience the challenge and fulfillment of participating in a hands-on ministry. Similarly, children involved in the church music program learn to appreciate all kinds of music and understand the important role of music in our worship experiences.

2. Musical productions at city theaters, schools, and churches introduce children to a wonderful world of rhythm and movement. Many children who are weak in social or even mental skills seem to come alive through music and dance. They learn to interpret meaning without a TV or movie screen in front of them. And they see what countless hours of practice and sacrifice mean to a performer. For many youngsters, music sets them free to dream, to feel, and to discover their bent.

3. Travel opportunities can open your child's mind to the world. Visit different scenery, historical monuments, and natural wonders. Understanding history has a unique way of linking us to the past, present, and future. It helps children feel connected in a very hurried, unconnected world. Natural wonders teach a new, awesome respect for the majesty and power of God. The beauty of nature is never forgotten and is the impetus for the creations of many songwriters, poets, playwrights, authors, and painters.

4. Museums and educational programs enlighten our young. Children's minds are continuously soaking in more and more information. A child who has a particular bent toward science or math thrives in places that stretch her or his analytical thinking skills. Building rockets, learning how light travels, taking apart a computer, or understanding the food chain process may be the beginning that unleashes your future physicist or engineer.

5. Interesting, age-appropriate lessons and activities—such as karate, dance, gymnastics, arts and crafts, tennis, bowling, swimming, and piano—broaden your child's horizons. Lessons can help your child learn the discipline required to master an interest or talent. If your child asks to take lessons, require him or her to practice and participate for a minimum of six months (if he or she is younger) or one year (if he or she is older). If you find that the lessons are causing your child emotional stress, re-evaluate according to your child's particular needs. Let your child know that after the set time period, you will discuss whether he or she should quit the lessons or try another activity.

At age seventeen, the Bruces' younger daughter, Ashley, is starting her twelfth year of piano and hopes to major in music in college. But as Robert recalls, there were some years when she was not an enthusiastic pianist:

Even as a young child, Ashley always had a bent toward music. However, when she hit middle school, she suddenly lost all interest in her musical studies. It seemed to happen overnight. One day she was laughing and playing a concerto; the next day she had tears in her eyes when she sat down to look at her assignments. Debra and I wondered, Do we let her quit or make her stick with this commitment? While we did not know the right answer, we weathered the stage. Her teacher suggested that we just let her enjoy playing the piano instead of expecting improvement. So, Ashley stayed in the same books all year, rarely practiced, and made little improvement. We agreed that if she would continue taking the lessons, she could progress at her own rate, hoping that interest would spark as she got older.

Sure enough, the next school year, she became our chameleon, going from hating the piano to falling in love with it once again. Now as she practices for hours each week and goes through difficult auditions for college scholarships, we know that we allowed her to lead the way in developing her talent.

6. People of all ages and cultures can help your child enhance his or her worldly perceptions. Senior adults add valuable perspective and wisdom to the way children and young adults look at life. Teenagers can also be positive mentors for young children. Likewise, people who haven't always had an easy life help to make all of us grateful for what we have.

Ellen's family especially enjoys befriending people from other countries. "We often host visitors to our city from other countries," reports Ellen. "We have learned so much about the rest of the world from them. As Americans, we dare to believe we have the 'corner on culture,' but by sharing their customs with us, our visitors have taught us to respect and admire their cultures."

One of the families Ellen and her family have hosted—the Ayanrinolas from Nigeria—have become their good friends. "The father, Duro, and his family are the most committed Christians we've ever known," Ellen says. "They truly understand and have modeled for us 'freedom in Christ.' Their journey is miraculous, though it has not been marked by wealth or ease. They remind us that all we have is a gift from God."

"I want my kids to have lots of good experiences, but I have no money," said Savannah, the mother of five active children. Sound familiar? How do we give our kids valuable experiences on a tight budget?

Allowing guilt to stifle your efforts because you do not have the time or money to offer certain experiences is wasted effort. Instead, think creatively of how you can expose your children to different experiences without spending much money. Your time and energy are free and can help to eliminate unnecessary guilt.

For example, if you can't afford to travel or buy camping equipment or you can't take time off from work, have a special family "camp-in" one Friday evening. Make a tent out of chairs, sheets, and blankets. Make a pretend fire out of sticks and construction paper, and serve hot dogs that you have pretended to cook over the fire. Serve hot chocolate with marshmallows for a special treat. Children enjoy any kind of adventure, especially if you enjoy it with them. A trip to an expensive amusement park is over in one day, but free weekend "camp-ins" build lifelong family memories.

Here's another idea. Ask a travel agency or airline ticket office for brochures on different countries. Look through them with your child and talk about the similarities and differences in clothing, hairstyles, climate, terrain, and transportation. Go to your local library and find books that tell of faraway countries. Make a list of foods brought over to America from other countries, such as frankfurters, tacos, pasta, and sauerkraut. Serve these at mealtime. You can decorate your dining area with the travel brochures, and invite your child's friends to an international gathering. Play background music from various countries, and let them taste foods such as rice (China), tortillas (Mexico), sauerkraut and frankfurters (Germany), curried fruit (India), and marzipan (Spain).

There are countless ways you can enrich your child's life—no matter how tight your budget. By doing so, you are enabling your child to reach into the depths of his or her being and discover those special interests he or she will use someday to give back to God's world.

Stay Active in Church

Perhaps no experience you might provide for your children does more to help them become all God intends them to be than participating in a church family. Being part of a spiritual community involves not only being cared for, but also caring for others. When we join a church or are confirmed, we make a commitment to be in service, to do God's work—which takes place within the church as well as at school, in our families, on the athletic field, and in community activities as we live our Christian discipleship each day. This service to others involves making our lives reflect Christ's spirit living in us. In other words, when we stay involved in the family of God, we teach our children how to put "feet to faith."

Church membership and commitment to a particular congregation also help our children to concretize their personal identities as they participate in worship services, Sunday school, other children's and youth programs, committees, choirs, and outreach activities—such as performing a skit for people who are unable to leave home or feeding the homeless. Not only are these acts of benevolence and giving self-rewarding for our children, who are finding their God-given talents and learning ways to express their thanks to God for these talents, but they also give our children much-needed confidence and acceptance. What's more, as our children and teens participate in the community of faith, they establish meaningful and necessary relationships with other Christian adults.

Encouraging our children to immerse themselves in the life of the church also helps them to develop a *personal faith.* Through Bible study, children gain an understanding of God's plan for our world and find help for answering their many questions regarding religious faith. And in time, through the experiences of prayer, worship, and fellowship with other Christians, they come to experience a personal relationship with the God who made them. As we have said, there is no parenting task more important than teaching our children about God and helping them to establish an abundant relationship with Him.

Value the Person, Not the Performance

The Scriptures remind us that *everything* we do to help our children "follow their own bent" and become all God intends them to be is well worth our time and effort. In Psalm 144:12, we read, "Then our sons in their youth will be like well-nurtured plants, / and our daughters will be like pillars carved to adorn a palace" (NIV). When our friend Sam read this verse, however, he told of feeling even more guilt. "I'm no gardener or sculptor, and my three children certainly do not resemble a botanical garden outside an ivory palace," he said. "How does this verse apply to busy parents trying to juggle jobs while raising kids?"

As we shared with Sam, the emphasis should be not on the plants and the pillars but on the words "well-nurtured" and "carved." As Christians, we are held accountable for the nurturing and carving, not for the garden or the palace. We all want our children to be people we can be proud of, yet if they grow up and make mistakes, sometimes our pride and embarrassment cause us to blame ourselves. This can easily happen if we focus on their trophies instead of their temperament. We may be tempted to measure our children's worth by how well they perform. The problem with this is that children get tired of performing, and perceptive teenagers recognize that their worth is determined by what they do—not by who they are.

Preschool experts caution teachers and parents to compliment children on their positive actions and qualities instead of attaching judgment words to their creativity or features. For example, rather than saying, "Kelly, you look so pretty in your new dress," say, "Kelly, I like how your new blue dress matches the color of your eyes." Or instead of saying, "John, don't do anything mean to hurt your brother," try saying, "John, I like it when you are kind to your brother. Thank you."

As children mature, they begin to perceive life's pressures to conform. They feel more and more of the world's pressures to look right, dress right, and behave according to the latest popular standards. How can you help? You can enable them to follow their "bent" by offering words of encouragement that do not measure their looks or accomplishments but reward their efforts, their hard work, their choice of clothing, or their choice of friends.

Author Neil Anderson tells a story about a seventeen-year-old girl who came to see him several years ago. Anderson said he never met a girl who had so much going for her: "She was cover-girl pretty with a wonderful figure. She was immaculately dressed. She had completed twelve years of school in eleven years, graduating with a grade point average of almost four. As a talented musician, she had received a full-ride music scholarship to a Christian university. And she drove a brand new sports car her parents gave her for graduation."

The teenager talked with Anderson for half an hour, and he began to realize that what he saw on the outside was not matching what he perceived to be on the inside. He finally said to her, "Mary, have you ever cried yourself to sleep at night because you felt inadequate and wished you were someone else?"

The girl began to cry and asked him how he knew. He said he

had learned that people who appear to have it all together are often far from being together inside. Anderson wrote:

> Often what we show on the outside is a false front designed to disguise who we really are and cover-up the secret hurts we feel about our identity. Somehow we believe that if we appear attractive or perform well or enjoy a certain amount of status, then we will have it all together inside as well. But that's not true. External appearance, accomplishment, and recognition don't necessarily reflect—or produce—internal peace and maturity.[3]

How important it is to value our children for who they are rather than for what they do, and to praise them for their efforts rather than for their accomplishments. When we do this, we are "nurturing and carving" our children well; we are enabling them to explore and experiment as they seek to find their own bent—without feeling guilty when they make mistakes or fail.

We Are the Gatekeepers

One Sunday morning years ago when Debra and Robert's daughter Brittnye was six years old, she grabbed both of their hands as they were leaving church and announced, "My Sunday school class smiles. And my teacher even knows my name." Brittnye's childlike interpretation of the affirmation that was shown to her by a caring adult was verbalized as being like a smile, making her feel happy, optimistic, and special.

As busy parents, we know how difficult it is to be cheerful and positive when days are filled with kids, car pools, chaos, and commitments. However, we are the gatekeepers of our homes, and as such we have daily opportunities to provide a "home that smiles."

Imagine for a moment a gatekeeper in biblical times keeping track of all the sheep—large and small, young and old—as they graze in the nearby pastures. If one sheep becomes lost or hurt along the way, the shepherd leaves the rest to find and comfort the sheep, helping it to regain strength to join the flock.

Sometimes in our dispassionate, technological culture, we may forget the compassion behind this image. In Jesus' day, a shepherd knew every sheep in the flock—its special habits, traits, and idiosyncrasies. He was able to predict the sheep's behavior under any condition or set of circumstances. He also was the one guiding light for many.

As modern-day gatekeepers, two of our main parenting tasks are to create a warm, positive environment and to know our children's habits and traits, so that they can respond with feelings of security and optimism about life. But how many times do negative actions and words tear down the positive spirit we are trying to cultivate?

Consider the following negative statements that many of us have used without thinking at one time or another:

* Why do you always look so sloppy?

* You act like a baby compared to your sister.

* What did I ever do to deserve a child like you?

* I hope you don't get that teacher next year. Who knows how she got certified?

* I can't wait to quit my job. I hate working.

* If the pastor doesn't wrap up this sermon soon, we'll miss the kickoff.

* Hurry and get that parking space before that other car does.

* That woman in the green van needs to go to driving school or get off the road.

And there are more. The irony is that most of us, no matter how hard we try to be positive, are guilty! Negative statements and actions have a tremendous impact on how children view the world. In other words, when children live in a home environment of careless cynicism and pessimism, they gain the attitude that life is out to get them.

No, life is not easy. But creating a warm, positive home is vital if we are to raise positive, self-confident children. As gatekeepers, we can role model the spiritual mind-set that our lives are on an eternal timetable, thus guiding our children to think and live in eternal realms.

Perhaps the following suggestions will enable you to become a positive gatekeeper in your home despite life's constant interruptions:

✓ Examine Your Words

Thoughts, feelings, and behaviors may mirror the soul, but the spoken word has the profound ability to build up or tear down your child. Recognizing that your words have a tremendous influence on your child's life and self-esteem, you should follow the example of Jesus Christ. He patiently listened to each person, empathized with his or her problems, and shared that selfless love with others while communicating a positive message of eternal truth.

✓ Watch Nonverbal Venom

Positive parenting communication does not mean just talking or listening; it includes nonverbal clues as well. Signals such as a slammed door, an unusual silence, and an irritable, sullen look can leave a venomous bite that stings deeper than words. To lay a positive foundation for your child, work on sharing concern and love with all of your signs, symbols, body language, and gestures.

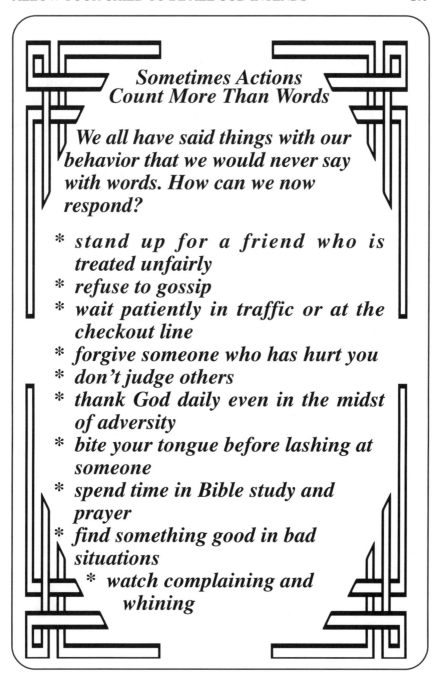

Sometimes Actions Count More Than Words

We all have said things with our behavior that we would never say with words. How can we now respond?

* *stand up for a friend who is treated unfairly*
* *refuse to gossip*
* *wait patiently in traffic or at the checkout line*
* *forgive someone who has hurt you*
* *don't judge others*
* *thank God daily even in the midst of adversity*
* *bite your tongue before lashing at someone*
* *spend time in Bible study and prayer*
* *find something good in bad situations*
  * *watch complaining and whining*

✓ *Live Agape Love*

Paul describes agape love as an active and vital force filled with compassion and empathy for others. Not only does it seek what is best for others, but it also sets out with unconditional caring to meet those needs. Agape love never changes; it continues to care, even when someone is broken, facing problems, ill, or acting unlovely.

✓ *Share Hugs—Not Criticism*

Though our society has been conditioned to be a hands-off society, hugs are the special key to ongoing, positive self-esteem. A pat on the shoulder after a firm reprimand, a loving hug after unlovely moments, or a caring back rub after a family quarrel is a positive way of letting your child know that you care. Often this loving touch can enable a negative parent to "bite her tongue" and replace anger with caring and sensitivity.

✓ *Advocate Tolerance*

Enable your child to develop tolerance for others through your example. Realize that each person develops at his or her own pace and is made in God's image. Talk with your child about the uniqueness of all people in God's world, and encourage acceptance of those who are different. As you show consideration for others, your child will learn to demonstrate tolerance of all people in his or her life.

We can nurture personal growth in our children as we make time to affirm them and role model positive actions and words based on biblical absolutes. Serving as gatekeepers in the home, we can empower our children to view life's challenges with hope and optimism, and encourage them to become the best they can be as they strive for eternal rewards. As you continue to evaluate your parenting attitude, keep in mind that your expectations and attitudes—no matter how positive or negative—greatly influence the path your child will take.

Plans of Hope

" 'For I know the plans I have for you,' declares the LORD, 'plans to prosper you and not to harm you, plans to give you hope and a future. Then you will call upon me and come and pray to me, and I will listen to you. You will seek me . . . with all your heart. I will be found by you . . . and will bring you back from captivity' " (Jer. 29:11-14 NIV). Are you helping your child to become all God intends without placing the demands of guilt on his or her life?

Start today to focus on your child's "bent"—the special direction that God has given to your child—and celebrate these talents together. Pray diligently that your child will gain a sense of God's direction for his or her life. Your own sensitivity to God in your life will enable you to see opportunities that will excite, challenge, and "grow" your child.

GUILT-FREE CHALLENGES

1. Even if you expose your child to every possible opportunity in an effort to understand his bent, you still would have ignored your most powerful tool. Sometimes we forget to pray for our children until they display some negative characteristic. Then in a harried panic, we run to God and seek help.

Pray for your child each day. If you have more than one child, pray for each child on a specific day. Make a list of the needs of each child and lift them up to the Lord. Ask God to lead you to someone who can be your prayer partner. Pray together with this person, and record your prayer requests along with God's answers.

2. To help you understand what impact varying persons and experiences can have on your child's development, recount your own early years. Who had an influence on your life? Who helped you to become what you are today? Even the bad influences helped shape your character. Thank God for the people who invested their time and love in your life. Write a thank-you letter to some of them.

If you have not completely dealt with the negative influences you experienced, ask God to help you put them in the proper perspective. Do you need to talk to someone about your past?

Think of special people who are investing time in your child's life right now. Write letters of appreciation to these people for helping to mold your child.

3. Sometimes we sit and wallow in our self-pity and guilt while making excuses for not getting out and experiencing

more of life. What excuses hold you back from celebrating your existence in God's world? Are you hiding behind your child? How can you overcome the obstacles that keep you buried in your "can't" instead of "can do" attitude? List some ways you can move out of negativism and into discovery. Number them in importance, and tackle one objective at a time.

4. Think intergenerational. What can your family do to get to know people of all ages? If you and your child do not have a relationship with a senior adult, you are missing an important ingredient in character development. Think of creative ways you and your child can be involved in an older person's life. If your time is too limited by forced constraints, try making a phone call periodically or developing a relationship through writing letters.

What type of relationship do you have with your parents? How does your child interpret this? Is there any action you need to take to nurture this relationship? Seek God's assurance as you work toward a more intimate tie with your family members.

5. The good news is that many parents are doing a great deal to allow their children to become all God intends. We affirm your selfless love and sacrifice, combined with commitment and diligence. Affirm yourself today! Write down at least five ways you are enabling your child to discover his or her "self" through your acceptance.

Chapter 9

Live Within Your Means

*A*s Christians, we are called to live within our means as we practice responsible stewardship, yet money—or the lack of it—adds fuel to the fire for many guilty parents. You may agree with one mother of three who told us, "No matter how much we make, we can't live on it." Personally, we know that nothing is more exasperating than paying bills only to realize that you have more month than money.

With more women working outside the home, two-income marriages are commonplace today. Yet financial matters continue to be the most common source of marital stress.[1]

The problem that tears couples apart is not necessarily the amount of money they have but their differing attitudes about that money. Single parents who have no choice but to seek a career outside the home in addition to the "career" of being Mom or Dad have their own financial worries. Money is certainly one issue that affects all our lives.

Will the Real Joneses Please Stand Up?

Dave Ramsey, president of a financial consultant group and radio talk show host, commented, "Only in America can you drive a Jaguar and not have the money to put gas in it." All it takes is a look around your community, your neighborhood, or even your own home to realize the truth of this statement

If you stay at home one evening, the odds are great that you will get a call about applying for a credit card. You can get them with your maiden name, your newborn's name, or even your dog's name. Credit cards, ATMs, national debt: America is money hungry and riddled with money problems. So, who is to blame? Where are those Joneses?

No, the name may not be "Jones." It may be your next-door neighbor, your boss, the parent sitting beside you in the pew at church, or your relative. The "Joneses" are the somebodies who buy and possess what we think we need or want. We assume money must not be a problem for them. We determine that their lifestyle is a pattern for success and if we emulate it, we, too, will become successful. That includes what they drive, where they live, what they wear, and where their children go to school—or preschool. Even if their kids participate in soccer, gymnastics, dance, and piano, we allow them to set the activity level and lifestyle pattern for our children.

In essence, we rob our own families of enjoying God's unique plan for our lives and teach them that creativity is to be copied and bought. And guess what creeps in when we can't financially or physically keep up with our real or imagined Joneses? The big *G* word takes over—GUILT—and the vicious cycle begins again.

Will the Circle Be Unbroken?

In his book *The Relaxed Parent,* Tim Smith warns parents that money cannot substitute for time.[2]

For families who equate success with more and bigger "stuff," money will dictate their lives. The more stuff you accumulate, the more time it takes to care for it. And it takes bigger and better stuff to meet your desires and compete with the Joneses.

In order to accumulate more and more, many parents work harder and longer. Children are given more stuff in an effort to make them happy and compensate for the time their parents cannot spend with them. Stuff initially makes children happy, but they soon learn to want more and more. Smith contends that it is not a parent's responsibility to make a child happy, and we agree.[3]

As a parent, you already know that children are born selfish. They demonstrate this characteristic in varying degrees as they learn how to manipulate those around them. As parents, we must help form their buying and spending patterns, along with their standards and Christian values. Our goal should be to raise responsible and independent children who will be able to contribute to their families, churches, and communities—children who have healthy self-esteem balanced with a genuine concern for others.

To do this takes time—and a lot of it. We must spend time helping them to develop a personal relationship with Jesus Christ and helping to nurture their growth as Christians. Hal Hadden, the president and founder of Christian Leadership Concepts, says that parents are to raise children who are independently dependent on God. To strive for that goal, we have to slow down, stop accumulating stuff, and become proactive in disciplining our own children.

Christian Stewardship and Tithing

We believe that Christian stewardship is a way of life, and Jesus is the perfect example for us to follow. Jesus used every moment of His life to glorify God; we are called to do the same.

We all enjoy the bounty of goods that God has provided. But everything—all that we have and are—belongs to God, including our earnings. God has made us the temporary trustees for His world; in fact, He gives us the power to receive these earnings (read Deut. 8:17-18).

The biblical guideline for giving to Christ's church is the tithe—10 percent of your income. It has been said that Christian stewardship and tithing are not the church's method for raising money but God's way of raising Christians! We affirm the tithe and have found that this important discipline has greatly deepened our faith and personal Christian commitment.

The Bible teaches us to set aside our firstfruits—not what is left over—to express love and gratitude for God's blessings. When you pay your tithe first—before anyone else is paid—and learn to live on the 90 percent left, that's responsible Christian stewardship.

After you have paid your tithe, pay yourself. Savings must also become a discipline that you do before you pay any bills as you learn to live on "enough." Whether you save 5 percent or 20 percent, save something, and live on the remaining amount. The rest of this chapter offers specific suggestions to help you do just that.

Distinguish "Needs" from "Wants"

Read 1 Timothy 6:6-10, and distinguish your family's "needs" from "wants." How much food, recreation, or clothing is "enough" in your home?

Evaluate Your Spending

A helpful exercise is to evaluate your spending habits. Ask yourself these questions about your latest (or next) purchases:

1. Is this a need or a want?

2. Do I want it to feel as successful as _____
   (fill in your "Joneses")?

3. If I make the purchase, will it keep our family from giving to the church or to others who are less fortunate?

4. Should I save the money instead of spending it?

5. How will this purchase help our family grow closer to each other and closer to God?

6. Will this purchase put us more in debt?

7. What am I teaching my children by making this purchase?

8. What am I telling others about my values?

Freeze Your Credit Cards

A continuously hefty credit card bill signals an inability to distinguish needs from wants. If your money and energy are wrapped up in a continuing debt spiral, you must stop the trend now. Using credit cards to buy everything means you don't have the money, you are paying more money in interest, and you are probably not saving any money. Providing your kids with a sprawling house in suburbia filled with the latest gadgets and toys, designer clothes, every lesson available, and fun-filled vacations is not wrong—unless it is keeping you from saving for their future or from teaching them to share with others. All three of us wish we had practiced more saving sense when our families were young so that we might be able to provide more for them now. You cannot put a college education—or your own retirement—on a credit card.

Stop the spiral now! Give up the cards. If you can't give them up, stick them in a bowl of water and freeze them! Letting go of unnecessary guilt involves disciplining yourself and your family to discern your needs from your wants and then provide the wants after you have saved for them. Each family member will appreciate the special things you have saved toward.

By freeing up your money from creditors, you are able not only to save for the future, but also to give in the present. Without debt you are free to reach out and help more people in need and give more to help your church share the love of Jesus Christ. Before your next large expenditure, stop and consider what Henry David Thoreau said: "Almost any man knows how to earn money, but not one in a million knows how to spend it."

Guilt-Free Steps to Control Spending

If you want to gain control of your family's funds, establish a deeper relationship with God, for He has the power to change your priorities. You also must take action, such as cutting up credit cards and limiting purchases to only the items budgeted that you can pay cash for. We have found that wearing less expensive clothes, grilling out instead of going out, and taking short trips close to home instead of annual trips to amusement parks before the kids are old enough to remember them can make a difference. After taking the following Controlled Spending List, turn to page 192 for some other ideas to help you gain control of your spending.

Do You Pass the Controlled Spending Test?

The National Center for Financial Education says the key to saving is controlling spending. The center's profile of a good spender is someone who:

_____ Saves a small amount of cash from each paycheck.

_____ Deposits money each payday into checking and savings accounts.

_____ Sets aside money for fixed expenses such as mortgages and 10 percent for savings.

_____ Sticks to a written spending plan.

_____ Plans all grocery shopping with a list, and rarely goes to the grocery store more than once a week.

_____ Uses grocery coupons.

_____ Comparison shops.

_____ Carries no credit card balances.

_____ Has no outstanding loans except a mortgage.

_____ Comparison shops auto insurance once a year.

_____ Dines out only once a week.

_____ Has received statements estimating Social Security and pension benefits.

_____ Can account for all cash spent at the end of each day.

_____ Belongs to a credit union.

_____ Automatically invests a set amount of money each month.

_____ Saves paycheck stubs.

_____ Gives regularly to the needy.[4]

20 Ways to Gain Control of Your Spending

1. Review the past year and list all of your expenditures. You will see that many purchases were spur-of-the-moment, impulsive decisions. Eliminate unnecessary spending by setting a budget and sticking to it. If you need to make monthly allotments for each category in your budget and put the money into separate envelopes marked for its use, then do it! Use only what you have allotted each month. Also budget a set amount for savings each month. When your debts are paid off—with the exception of your mortgage and possibly one car note—and you have begun to save for emergencies, future expenses, and your children's education, then you can start making the "fun" envelope a little bigger.

2. Make a shopping list and ask yourself, Do I really need this? Stick to your list.

3. Clip coupons, but don't rush to purchase just because you have the coupon. Do you really need it? Compare it with store brands.

4. Shop wholesale clubs for larger quantities and save up to 30 to 40 percent.

5. Buy clothes at end of season and on sale when possible.

6. Shop discount department stores and factory outlets, always comparing quality and price. You will find the more an item is advertised, the more it costs.

7. Shop garage sales in higher income neighborhoods when possible. Many times you will find high-quality children's clothes at one-tenth of the retail price.

8. Shop thrift shops. Many times you can find clothing, appliances, and furniture in excellent condition at low cost.

9. Custom make your children's clothes. Take a sewing course and find out how easy it is.

10. Contact your utility company and request an energy audit. Many companies will do this for no charge or for no more than a few dollars. Some will even offer a rebate if you will upgrade to a more efficient heating and cooling system. Insulate your water heater and check into the possibility of using a timer to heat water only when you need it. Become aware of the energy efficiency of all appliances. Install water-saving shower heads and aerators.

11. Look at your automobiles. The family that buys top-of-the-line cars every three years is making a costly mistake by keeping up with the Joneses. Sam Walton, one of the richest men in our country, was famous for sporting around town in his used pickup truck. Tremendous savings may be possible if you will review your transportation needs. Consult *Consumer Reports* before purchasing a car; in fact, you should check this source before all major purchases.

You may decide to have only one family car, and other family members may use public transportation. Or you may purchase a low mileage car. A new car drops in value up to 30 percent when it is driven off the dealer's lot. Today most dealers have program cars with low mileage at up to 35 percent off the ticket price, and they offer discounts off current models with several years of factory warranty left. Compare these options with a new car, and negotiate the price and interest rate. After several years, the older car can become the second car.

Consider driving it for as long as it provides sound transportation.

12. Take advantage of the many opportunities your church offers for fellowship. Covered dish meals, youth fellowship, church camp, retreats, Sunday school parties, singles fellowship, and more are free and will help you grow in your Christian commitment. We compared summer camps and found our denomination's youth camp was one-fourth the cost of a private camp. Both camps were in the same area and offered the same activities, but the church camp also had a spiritual emphasis.

13. Consider vacations at church recreation facilities. Most denominations have various campgrounds and retreat centers available for members.

14. Review insurance coverage with your agent and consider increasing your deductibles on auto, homeowners, or renters up to $250, $500, or more.

15. If you are working part-time, consider a child care co-op with other parents who work part-time. Schedule your work to make the co-op work and save the cost of day care.

16. Take advantage of the many inexpensive software programs to assist in personal financial planning and budgeting. If you are not computer literate, ask a friend or relative to help you get started.

17. Explore the availability of purchasing food through co-ops at your church or with neighborhood groups.

18. Make meals from scratch; reduce prepared dishes; minimize restaurant meals and call-in pizzas.

19. When these changes are not enough, consider lifestyle

changes. Move to a smaller house or plan for additional education to qualify for a more lucrative position.

20. Subscribe to a magazine that offers tips on money management. *Consumer Reports* and *Money* magazine are worth considering. Some excellent resources for financial management include Larry Burkett's *Answers to Your Family's Financial Questions*; Jane Bryant Quinn's *Making the Most of Your Money*; and Joe Dominguez and Vicki Robin's *Your Money or Your Life.*[5]

Financial consultant Dave Ramsey emphatically states that there is no way around it: You must figure out what your income is and then live *below* this amount.[6]

Now that doesn't mean you have to "sell the farm" and apply for government housing. It does mean that you must seek alternative buying and spending methods, stick with these methods, and teach your children how to save money and live on a frugal budget.

Make Saving a Family Affair

Teaching your children how to save money can be a fun and rewarding experience for the whole family. If your family wants to take a big vacation, for example, plan it two years ahead. Decide together how you will save for it and create savings methods for each family member. Then make a fun "diagram" that shows how much you have saved each month. Say you want to go to a theme park. After determining how much money it will take, let your kids draw a big picture of the state you will travel to and color in a small part of it for each one hundred dollars saved. When the state is completely colored, you are ready to go!

Several years ago, Ellen's family wanted to go to a popular family resort and recreation park. To help earn money for the trip, they held a family garage sale. Every member "donated" items, tagged them, and took shifts at the sale. From their earnings they were able to pay for their passes and provide spending money. They worked together to save and to spend.

One mother tells of making savings banks out of coffee cans and placing them in an easy-to-see place in their home. One can is marked for vacation or a big-ticket item the family really wants, and one is marked for college. Family members are not forced to put in money, but this young mother and her husband have set an example for their children. Now everyone wants to contribute. The parents put in loose change and rebates, and the kids freely put in extra earnings, gifts, and portions of their allowance.

Decide What Is Most Important

Financial advisor Larry Burkett has said that with so many easily available borrowing opportunities, today's young couples can quickly have the same lifestyle it took their parents twenty-five years to achieve. They may even have newer cars and nicer clothes than their parents, who make more money and have worked their whole adult lives to attain what they have.[7]

The problem is that what many young couples now have that their parents did not is debt—simply because they could not wait. They couldn't make purchases the "old-fashioned" debt-free way. They couldn't say "no" to themselves, to their children, or to the Joneses.

Ending parenting guilt means sorting through your value system and making firm priorities for your family. For example, is it more important to help your children get a good college education or for them to wear designer clothes to church and preschool? Is it more important for them to find one thing they enjoy and can excel in or to be involved in three sports, two dance classes, and karate so that you can brag about how busy your children are?

Blink your eyes three times really fast and you will know what it feels like when they have grown. As parents of teens and young adults, we know how time zooms by, regardless of how much you try to cram into their lives or how much their clothes cost. Your children will be grown, and you will be faced with what you have or have not taught them about how to deal with life and how to grow in Christ.

The decision is yours. It is not fair for children to decide or to dictate. Quite honestly, they will remember very little about how many matching dresses and hair bows they owned or how many bicycles and trampolines they possessed before age six. But they will remember how much time you spent with them. They will translate your love into whether you were there or not. Do you want them to playfully complain that they always had to wear sale clothes? Or would you rather they sit in a counselor's office and cry that you never spent time with them?

Financial choices are difficult choices to make, and it is especially hard for single parents. Many single parents try to ease the guilt of divorce by providing more "stuff" for their children. Stuff is a cheap substitute because quantity and quality time is expensive. Instead of worrying over the stuff, expose your kids to families who can have a positive influence on their lives.

Ellen tells about some friends who went the second mile when she was a single parent:

My son, Stuart, got his first non-clip-on tie. He was so proud of it, and he was going to wear it on Easter Sunday. I had bought him a new shirt and pictured how grown up he would look. What I didn't picture was how to tie the recently purchased non-clip-on tie!

We were blessed to have a single adult minister at our church who really cared about us and showed it. I called him, and he graciously and quietly met us at church and tied Stuart's tie. Then he set a time to come over to our house and work with Stuart until he could master the art of tie tying. Through many other demonstrations of love, he and his wife made a lasting impression on our family.

If you are a single parent or your children are living in a situation that is lacking a positive influence from both parents, ask God to bring some friends or teachers into your life who can help you give your children what they really need. Stuff won't do it. It's always temporary.

Presents or Presence?

Learning to be a "good enough" parent means limiting the material gifts you provide for your child. Many parents, especially working parents, find that giving special gifts after a long day at day care or the sitter's house makes them feel less guilty for being away from their children. It does not have to be this way. Parents who overcompensate with material gifts because of lack of time are really being too generous, which can result in greedy children.

Children who receive too many material gifts will continue to demand material gifts. You set the trend. A simple coloring book and crayons at age four turn into TV sets, VCRs, CD players, and new cars at age sixteen. Of course, the choice is up to you. If you want to surprise your children with gifts, you can. But remember to ask yourself if you are giving gifts because of your children's need or your want. If you are providing for your children's physical, emotional, and spiritual health and well-being, if they have nutritious meals and a clean bed to sleep in and are reasonably happy, you are being a good enough parent.

No one can draw the line in your home but you. Take it from parents who have been there: Your presence will leave a much greater impression on your children than any present. Give hugs, not toys!

The Bottom Line

We would not begin to pretend that family budgeting is an easy issue. Financial burdens can rob you and your family of the very best God intended. The hope lies in God's concern and compassion. Right now, God is calling you to be proactive—proactive parents with proactive pocketbooks.

Is it time to have the "big talk" in your family? Not about the facts of life, but about the finances of life. As we have experienced, you will have to make some sacrificial decisions, but it will be worth it.

Ellen and her husband, John, became convinced several years ago that they were headed in the wrong direction. Ellen admits that John became convicted faster than she did and has kept them on the right track with more diligence. John's motivation increased as he read books by Christian financial consultants and researched information in financial and consumer magazines.

First, they threw away their credit cards and vowed never to purchase anything on credit. They listed their debts and began to pay them off, from the one with the most interest to the one with the least. When one debt was paid off, its monthly amount was rolled into the next debt. Then they budgeted for everything else. When the debts were paid off, savings increased. Now they watch their ATM withdrawals and use a debit check card that can be used like a credit card but comes directly out of their checking account. They still enjoy special treats, such as going out to eat to celebrate a special achievement or grabbing a pizza for family night. But if it jeopardizes the budget, then they cut back on spending in other areas for that month.

Ellen admits that it gets old to evaluate every purchase, but that the rewards are worth it. "It's much more fun to open sweepstakes envelopes than bills," she says. "Now we are getting more letters from Ed McMahon than the bank!"

The Bruces also found out the hard way that setting parenting priorities and budgeting are vital for healthy Christian families. Sixteen years ago, with both parents working, eating out each night seemed like the convenient and "easy" way to go, especially when compared to cooking meals for three hungry preschoolers after working long hours. Debra shares:

> This "easy" way out was also expressed in excessive spending on "stuff"—expensive clothes, toys, and gadgets—stuff that none of us needed or used. After living this way from month to month, it became apparent that our combined salaries were not necessary for a balanced lifestyle—the extra money that I was making was used to pay for excessive fun. We realized that we were caught in the trap of wanting it all—but giving up what was most important to have this.
>
> With some tight budgeting, I was able to stop working outside the home and begin a home-based business, writing while the kids were in preschool. After-school time was spent teaching, talking, and enjoying time with our three little ones. Dinners were homemade and eaten around the family table. And without the latest "wind-up" toys, our children began to use their minds to invent their own "stuff" to play with.
>
> Have we suffered? Not at all. What we lost in dollars, we gained in teaching our children and knowing that we were doing what was best for their growth and development.

If you bought your child a special toy and he played with it for a few days and then left it outside in the rain, how would you feel? You probably would hesitate to entrust him with another new toy for a while. You certainly would feel disappointed that he did not care enough about you to be careful with the gift you gave him.

How do you think God feels when He so graciously shares His blessings and gifts with us, and we "play" with them awhile and then leave them out in the rain? God wants us to manage the resources He provides.

Treat God's blessings with care and gratefulness. God provides because He loves you.

GUILT-FREE CHALLENGES

1. Make sure extended family members understand your commitment to careful spending and responsible stewardship. Sometimes grandparents will want to fund your vacation or big ticket item instead of understanding that you and your children are waiting until the money is saved. Explain to relatives what you are trying to teach your children and how you hope this experience will benefit them as they grow up.

2. As your children reach school age and receive allowances and earn extra money, take them to the bank and open a savings account. Help them keep up with their money, and take them to the bank often to help them understand the banking process. When they become teenagers and show interest in buying more or earning money, take them to the bank and open a checking account. Emphasize, repeat, and "paint on their ceilings" the dangers of credit cards.

3. Expose your family to people of different cultures and backgrounds. After spending an evening with someone from a country with fewer conveniences or the problems of war, talk with your children about how fortunate and blessed they are. Lead your family in prayer for missionaries from your church or denomination. Learn about their countries and special needs, and discuss what you might do in response.

4. Have a garage sale, and use the money for a special family activity or give it to a special cause. If garage sales take too much time, simply sort out clothes that don't fit anymore and give them to an agency that helps the needy. Involve your children in this benevolent act, and talk about the feelings they have when they help those who are not as fortunate in life.

5. Don't be a "Jones family wanna-be." If you are obsessed with spending time with those who seem to have it all, you are missing out on some great rewards. Spend time with friends who also are trying to live debt-free and are using their resources to reach out to others. That will encourage you to live within your means. Form a financial support group, and share ideas about how to save.

Chapter 10

Know When to Let Go

I did all I could to raise decent kids," the mother of two young adults said, "but I must have gone wrong somewhere because they don't listen to anyone but their friends."

This mother went on to tell how her two girls quit junior college after just a few weeks, then drove around the country searching for thrills. "They finally ended up living with some boys they met in another state. It breaks my heart to think about what they could have done with their lives."

A father whose twenty-year-old son spent the past year in jail for check fraud and robbery also blamed himself for the boy's history of delinquency, saying, "When he was in elementary school, he was such a loner. I should have known then to get him some professional help. Now it's too late."

Another single mother told of being disappointed that her teenage son chose to take vocational classes at school instead of the college preparatory curriculum. "I had always hoped he would be a doctor because he is so good with his hands," she said, "but he wants to be a mechanic."

We all have hopes and dreams for our children, whether it is to be the gifted scholar, athlete, or musician. However, sometimes we fail to comprehend that our children also have their own ideas about what they want to do with their lives—ideas that are sometimes quite the opposite of our well-intentioned plan.

If you think it is difficult to ease parenting guilt while your children are young, consider how you will feel when they are no longer in your command. Can we parents let our children go *without guilt,* especially when we know that as older teens and young adults they could make mistakes with their life choices? We believe we can!

Caring enough to let go involves letting your child fail and make mistakes, even at a young age, then opening your arms in love when the child comes running home. There is a significant difference between "caring" for children and always "taking care" of them, as we will explore.

We have experienced that many wonderful parents watch in despair as their young adults experiment with lifestyles that are not Christian. When this occurs, the bond between parent and child is strained to the breaking point. These are some of the most guilt-ridden feelings a parent can experience. Not only are the parents disappointed by the child's poor choices, but they also wonder how they could produce a child who could be so different from them.

No matter what choices a child makes, guilt-free parents must remain constant. As in the story of the prodigal son, parents are commissioned to teach God's way, then let go. If the child goes astray, we should know that we did all we could to help mold him, then wait with loving, caring arms outstretched to welcome the child when he comes to his senses and asks to come home. At this time, parental love can help to heal and mend the broken young life.

Even as we treasure precious moments with our children, we know a day will come when we will not make decisions for them. With children in high school, college, and graduate school, Robert and Debra have watched their children make choices apart from the family—what courses to take, what people to befriend, what boyfriends and girlfriends to choose, and what careers to gravitate toward. As the Bruce children have moved out into the world, Robert and Debra have given them God's blessings—*without guilt*—knowing that they have done all they could to prepare them for the real world.

"We worked for years to help them to grow in wisdom and grace so we could let go in complete trust and faith," Debra shares. "This is what Christian parenting is all about. Faith in a loving God who gives strength and guidance enables us to let go in love."

Letting Go Starts Early

As our children become older and begin to make their own decisions, we really have little choice in the matter of letting go. But letting go actually begins much earlier.

Debra recalls that when she was in the hospital with her first-born son, Rob, she wanted to hold him and get to know him but had to wait as others played a key role in his young life. "I wanted so much to be with my son," she recalls, "but rooming-in was not vogue two decades ago. Instead, I had to accept only those precious, brief moments during feeding time to have my newborn all to myself."

Even when our children are only minutes old, many other people are vital to their development, providing nurture and care. The night nurse who diligently rocks the newborn during those fussy moments becomes more important than Mother at that moment, as does the hospital volunteer who keeps the baby clean and dry during the day. Even the pediatrician who registers the vital signs as the baby makes his or her debut becomes a most important "other" in the child's new world.

"But wait," you might interject. "I'm the child's mother. I am the one who carried him for nine months, who labored for hours to present him to the world, who prepared the perfect environment to take him home to. You're saying that others are already important in my child's life?" Yes, even prior to birth we must get used to not being the only persons in our child's life and learn to let go of the gift we so selfishly call "mine."

Letting Go Can Be "Unexpected"

We find ourselves having to let go at the most unexpected times—when a loved one dies suddenly, when someone suffers a lingering illness in the prime of life, when our babies mature into toddlerhood as we watch them take their first step, or when we help our children onto the school bus for the first time. Yet when we realize that letting go is inevitable and accept it as a reality of life, the pain is less piercing.

Robert tells of the time when Ashley, then age six, walked down the crowded halls to her first-grade classroom:

I remember asking the student in the patrol uniform if I could escort her to class, but he shook his head emphatically. Then he quoted the rule in the PTA handbook that "all adults must check into the main office to receive a permission slip to go into a classroom." I could hardly stand it! Here was my baby, my youngest child, leaving for the entire day, and these patrols had orders to hold back parents. The irony of the situation was that Ashley didn't even turn around or appear timid, but approached the new experience in her life with complete confidence.

No one ever said that letting go is predictable or easy. To watch our children break away and become independent is painful. These same human beings who once were dependent on us struggle out into the cruel world. Yet we must remember that letting our children "go and grow" throughout childhood is part of their inevitable journey into responsible adulthood. As the parent-child bond becomes fragile and thin, the dependent relationship develops first into one of independence and then into one of interdependence and love.

Walking the Tightrope

After working late several days in a row, Valerie took off early one afternoon to enjoy a shopping trip at the mall with her daughter, Meagan. As they hurried from one store to another, taking advantage of the bargains, Meagan saw a friend from her middle school. "Let Meagan come home with us for the afternoon," the girl's mother generously offered.

"Please, Mom," Valerie's twelve-year-old pleaded lovingly. Then seeing the disappointment in her mother's eyes as the two ended their special mother-daughter shopping trip, Meagan added, "You wait for me, and we can talk tonight." Valerie never told anyone that she cried that afternoon.

Letting go often involves caring more for the needs of others than for our own. Meagan's need to be with a friend, to experience the fantasies and laughs that only two preteens can share, outweighed Valerie's motherly need to be with her.

We have realized through personal experiences and our observations of others that trying to keep children dependent only soothes and comforts the parents. This strong parental dependence often hinders children's maturity and development. We have found, on the other hand, that allowing our children to participate in school activities, youth choirs, teams, and enrichment classes has enabled them to grow and develop. We have often reminded ourselves of this as we have waited patiently in long car pool lines with other caring parents!

As parents, we often have to walk a fine line between giving our children the necessary freedom to become independent and knowing when to hold them back with parental protection. Children who are overprotected may rebel in later years or become overly dependent on their parents. Children *need* interaction with peers and opportunities to make their own decisions.

Believing that his teenage daughter needed him more than peer interaction, Ben kept a firm grip on her by continuing to plan extra activities, limiting her social environment, and "selecting" only the friends he felt were acceptable. Ben mistakenly made all the decisions for his child during her breaking away years rather than giving her some leeway to make friends and decisions on her own.

Now in her midteens, the girl has found a new freedom— opposite of what her father dreamed. She is sneaking out of the house at all hours of the night, choosing peers with values unlike her own, and defying her parents' rules and standards. By refusing to let go of his daughter through the years, Ben may have stimulated her rebellion in the teen years.

As we have said, caring enough to let go involves letting a child fail and make mistakes, then opening your arms in love when the child comes running home. As you help to pick up the pieces, you are enabling him to grow through the failure.

Let Go and Let God

As loving parents, most of us want to help our children grow through failure. But how do we cope with the guilt that often accompanies a child's failures? What do we do with our own emotions when a child takes a less desirable direction in life?

In Native American culture, one way of dealing with emotional pain is to dig a hole in the ground, lie down on your stomach, and speak loudly into the hole, releasing all your negative thoughts as well as your fears, frustrations, discouragement, and anger. Then you are to cover the hole with dirt and "bury" the stressful emotions.

Perhaps this would be a good exercise for guilty parents who have a difficult time letting go. We need to take our guilt and shame and cast them into the sea or bury them in the ground. After all, if a holy God can forgive us, surely, it is time for us to forgive ourselves.

A pastor-friend, Peter, told of the torment his youngest son put the family through during his teenage years:

> Jonathan was always a mischievous child, but during his teen years he seemed to attract trouble. If a teacher wasn't calling to say he was skipping school, the neighbors were pounding on the front door, saying he had egged their house or chased their dog in his car. We didn't know how to react. We had worked hard to be good parents, and our other three kids turned out to be respectful citizens.
>
> The day after high school graduation, Jonathan left home, and we didn't hear from him until months later. We would get cards in the mail periodically, but with no return address. For several years, his mother and I worried endlessly and virtually blamed ourselves for his actions.
>
> About four years after he ran away, our son finally returned home as a man. He had joined the Marines and loved it and was stationed about one hour away from our home. With tears in his eyes, Jonathan asked us if we could ever forgive him for causing so much pain to the family. We were so glad that our son had come home that we could hardly remember what we had been through for eighteen long years.

Are you willing to lay aside the past with your child and focus on today—this moment? Are you ready to say that you have done all you could as a Christian parent to raise this child? Are you willing to let go and let God?

Pray Without Ceasing

The psalmist says, "Evening and morning and at noon I utter my complaint and moan, and he will hear my voice" (Ps. 55:17 RSV). Prayer does change things! If there is a broken relationship in your family, prayer can help to unite family members and can give purpose to the problem at hand.

In our own homes, prayer is the one strength we can lean on when our children are out of control. That special communication enables the difficult child to know of God's love and power, even when the enthusiasm is not felt. And prayer can be the peaceful serenity a distraught parent needs during moments of anguish.

Practice Forgiveness

Forgiveness offers permission to see mistakes as opportunities for learning and growing. The whole message of the Gospels lies

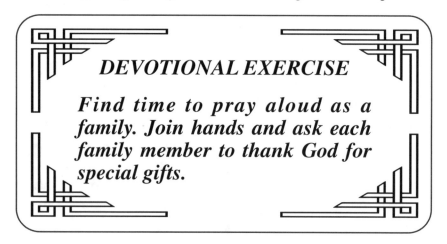

DEVOTIONAL EXERCISE

Find time to pray aloud as a family. Join hands and ask each family member to thank God for special gifts.

in loving and forgiving. Yet who hasn't harbored feelings of anguish that accompany parenting guilt?

As we continually place our faith in God and build our lives around His Word, we can experience the strength to forgive our children and move beyond past trials. This agape or selfless love becomes a reality as we generate acceptance, forgiveness, and growth, and as we place our ultimate faith in the person of Jesus Christ instead of in humankind.

Through personal quiet times, prayer, Bible study, and fellowship with other Christians, you can acknowledge God's presence and know yourself to be loved for who you are—not for how perfect you are or what you do or how much money you make or how perfect you or your children appear to others.

Face Darkness Triumphantly

If you have been a parent for years, you know that life does not move on a level plain. You have experienced the hills and valleys of life and need someone to help level them out. For Jesus, after the mountaintop experience of hearing the voice of God calling, "Thou art My beloved Son," came the valley of the temptation of Satan. After victory, Jesus also found Himself in the wilderness of darkness.

Then we see Jesus in the garden. Few other scenes in the Gospel story have been the source of such strength and comfort as this one. For Jesus, facing His darkest hour with feelings of loneliness and fear, God is intimate and close. Rather than letting His troubles drive a wedge between Him and the Father, Jesus chose to let them bring Him closer to God.

Parenting is not easy, especially today. For even the best parents, it is a constant marathon with many obstacles. Being Christians does not mean that the way will be made smooth for us. Our children will rebel. They may defy us, our values, and our Lord. They may face failure, tragedy, and sorrow. We will watch our children suffer. We will grieve the loss of their dreams and future hopes. At such times, we must have faith for the long term.

Although our heavenly Father has promised to be with us always, He never promised to remove us from the trials of life. Indeed, God sometimes delivers us from a situation only when the circumstances of that situation seem to be beyond our hope.

Finish the Race

The great secret in being a guilt-free parent is not how we begin, but how we finish. You see, most parents are good starters. They have wonderful goals for their tiny child, along with enthusiasm for how they will raise that child. Most parents start out with a burst of "well-doing" when their precious baby is born. But sustaining that enthusiasm and commitment to the end is a problem.

Are you committed to the finish line? That is the test of a guilt-free parent. When the enthusiasm fades, when the child becomes independent, when his or her grades drop, when the rebellion begins and wrong choices are made, are you still hanging in?

Faith means hanging in there when the day looks dark and the options are limited, because you know that somewhere out there is coming the victory of God. You may not experience this for yourself—at least not this side of the grave—but you know it is coming. Thus, you place your child in God's hands and trust that He will take care of him.

This is our faith at its best, and guilt-free parenting demands that you have this unending faith. We believe that it is not how you start the parenting race that matters, but how you finish.

As you treasure precious moments with your family today, it is important to realize that the day will come when you will not make decisions for them. Your children will grow up, choose their own mates and careers, then move out into the world on their own.

Do not be disheartened! Continue in the parenting marathon, yet pray that you shall grow in wisdom and grace so when the time comes, you can let go in complete trust and faith. This is what Christian parenting is all about. Remember, faith in a loving God who gives strength and guidance enables guilt-free parents to let go in love.

NOTES

1. The Verdict: Guilty or Not Guilty?

1. Cecil Osborne, *Release from Fear and Anxiety* (Waco, Tex.: Word Books, 1976), 130.
2. Marjorie Hansen Shaevitz, *Super Woman Syndrome* (New York: Warner, 1984), 39.

2. Good Guilt/Bad Guilt

1. Joan Borysenko, "Ridden with Guilt," *Health* (March 1990): 68-71.

4. Peace Is a Person

1. A. W. Tozer, *The Pursuit of God* (Carp Hill, Penn.: Christian Publications, 1982).
2. Ray C. Stedman, *Authentic Christianity* (Portland, Oreg.: Multnomah Press, 1975), 155.

6. Prevent Parenting Burnout

1. *Webster's New Collegiate Dictionary* (Springfield: G. & C. Merriam, 1973).
2. Gordon MacDonald, *Ordering Your Private World* (Nashville: Thomas Nelson, 1985), 13.
3. Ibid., 31-33.
4. Tim and Darcie Kimmel, *Little House on the Freeway* (Sisters, Oreg.: Multnomah Books, 1994), 1.

7. Set Priorities and Goals

1. Gini Kopecky, "What Do You Really Want Out of Life?" *Family Circle* (January 1996): 6.
2. Elaine V. Emeth, "Time Management as Spiritual Discipline," *Kaleidoscope* (June-July 1995): 31-33.

8. Allow Your Child to Be All God Intends

1. Jay Kesler, *Ten Mistakes Parents Make with Teenagers* (Brentwood, Tenn.: Wolgemuth & Hyatt, 1988), 58.
2. George Barna, *The Future of the American Family* (Chicago: Moody Press, 1993), 17.
3. Neil T. Anderson, *Victory Over the Darkness* (Ventura: Regal Books, 1990), 18.

9. Live Within Your Means

1. George Barna, *The Future of the American Family* (Chicago: Moody Press, 1993), 58.
2. Tim Smith, *The Relaxed Parent* (Chicago: Northfield, 1996), 24.
3. Ibid., 48.
4. "Good Spenders," *Florida Times-Union* (February 13, 1994): G-1.
5. Robert and Debra Bruce, *Reclaiming Your Family* (Nashville: Broadman & Holman, 1994), 211.
6. Dave Ramsey, *Financial Peace* (Nashville: Lampo Press, 1995), 58.
7. Ibid.